Building Societies in the Financial Services Industry

Barbara Casu • Andrew Gall

Building Societies in the Financial Services Industry

palgrave
macmillan

Barbara Casu
Faculty of Finance
Cass Business School-City University
London, United Kingdom

Andrew Gall
Building Societies Association
London, United Kingdom

ISBN 978-1-137-60207-7 ISBN 978-1-137-60208-4 (eBook)
DOI 10.1057/978-1-137-60208-4

Library of Congress Control Number: 2016942676

Printed on acid-free paper

This Palgrave Macmillan imprint is published by Springer Nature
The registered company is Macmillan Publishers Ltd. London

Foreword

Building societies and, indeed, the mutual concept itself were written off by many in the late 1990s. Those societies that saw themselves as innovative, risk-taking, and entrepreneurial had proudly cast away what they saw as the constraints of their mutual status. By 2000, they were ready to take their full and rightful role in the new, free, globalised financial markets that had been created by new technology and regulatory reform over the previous two decades.

A decade later, the ambition, excitement, and sense of self-belief among those who led this change had disappeared. By 2009, not a single one of the ten building societies that had turned themselves into banks retained their individual existence, and a number had been rescued by the taxpayer. In contrast, most of those societies that remained mutual, and fought to reinvent and enhance the meaning of mutuality, survived the financial crisis, and came out of it stronger. One of the most remarkable statistics in this welcome new book by Barbara Casu and Andrew Gall is that between 2011 and 2014, mutual building societies accounted for 90% of net new mortgage lending.

The history of this period is fascinating, and Casu and Gall provide a range of insights. The wealth of data in this book means it is set to become a standard statistical text on developments in this area. However, the authors go further, with helpful interpretations and analysis of market developments, financial performance, and customer views. The impact of regulatory change is not ignored; indeed, it is explained in some detail. It is interesting to reflect that, to some extent, the country chose to go down a route that led to such ruin.

Vince Cable, Liberal Democrat Business Secretary in the 2010–2015 coalition government, said that the demutualisations had been “one of the great acts of economic vandalism in modern times.” That statement deserves sustained reflection by policymakers and those who drive market behaviour. The huge and costly experiment to determine whether mutual or stock-based ownership models are best designed to provide customers with basic financial products has been comprehensively answered in mutuals’ favour in recent years. Those wanting to understand “how” and “why” should spend a few hours with “Building Societies in the Financial Services Industry.”

Adrian Coles
Director General, The Building Societies
Association, 1993–2013

Preface

The UK financial services industry has been severely impacted by the financial crisis of 2007–2008, which resulted in UK banks suffering big losses. The financial turmoil resulted in significant government intervention in the sector. State aid was then followed by wide-ranging regulatory reforms, aimed at making the financial industry more resilient to shocks, by limiting risk-taking and improving bank conduct. As a consequence, the industry is undergoing a period of deep transformation, which affects all industry participants.

The implications of the global financial crisis on the banking sector have been widely analysed, less so the consequences on other financial intermediaries. Not all types of financial institutions were affected in the same way by the crisis.

Although the building society sector was not immune to the effects of the global financial crisis, on average, it managed to overcome it in better health than the banking industry.

An analysis of the key characteristics of the UK building society sector is therefore interesting to understand how different types of financial institutions have evolved during the deregulation era of the 1990s, when activity restrictions were abolished and banks and building societies started competing in the mortgage and savings markets, and how this affected the range of activities undertaken in the run-up to the financial crisis.

Building societies are mutual organisations, owned by their customers, or members. Although technically they are not "banks" and do not offer the full range of banking services, as mutuals they are a subset of stakeholder-based financial institutions. Understanding the key features of their business models and analysing their strengths and weaknesses compared to banks are particularly interesting as policymakers are seeking to foster a more diverse financial sector. In recent years, building societies have enjoyed political support as the importance of mutuals within a more diverse financial sector has been highlighted by policymakers and regulators. This support is also recognised by customers, as indicated by the high levels of satisfaction and trust.

This book aims to describe the performance of UK building societies since the large-scale demutualisation process ended in the year 2000. Chapter 1 offers an overview of the UK financial services industry and reviews the impact of the global financial crisis on UK banking. It also provides an analysis of the changing structure of the UK banking sector: from increased concentration, which resulted in the sector being dominated by few, very large, banking groups to the recent entrance of new "challenger" banks. The entrance of new banks, with new banking licences being issued for the first time in a century, is likely to increase competition, particularly in the retail banking sector. This increased competition, in addition to the effect of regulatory reforms, as well as far-reaching technological innovations, presents new challenges for the building society sector. Chapter 2 presents a brief summary of UK building societies' 250 years of history. We focus in particular on the demutualisation process that saw the largest building societies becoming banks. We then assess the impact of the financial crisis on the sector; we analyse the consolidation process that took place as larger and more sound building societies took over troubled ones. Chapter 3 reviews the legal and regulatory framework with respect to building societies' permissible activities and discusses recent developments. In addition, we consider the strengths and weaknesses of the building society model, with a particular focus on capital and governance. Chapter 4 presents an analysis of the key issues faced by building societies in today's financial markets. We discuss the key changes in the structure of the industry and how these have impacted on margins and profitability and have resulted in restructuring and consolidation in the sector. Finally, Chapter 5 presents an empirical analysis of the comparative performance of UK banks and building societies since the year 2000. When comparing societies against standard bank performance metrics, we have been careful in the interpretation of the results not to provide a biased view of the sector's performance. We believe this analysis to be informative to demonstrate the differences between types of organisations competing in the market and therefore helpful to policymakers weighing up the future shape of the banking sector.

Barbara Casu
Faculty of Finance, Cass Business School, City University London, UK

Andrew Gall
Building Societies Association, London, UK

Acknowledgements

This text could have never been completed without the help and support of a number of individuals. First and foremost, the authors must acknowledge the financial support of the Building Societies Association (BSA). The results of the empirical analysis presented in Chapter 5 are part of a Report commissioned by the BSA to the Centre for Banking Research at Cass Business School. The Report titled *An analysis of the comparative performance of UK banks and building societies* was presented at the BSA London offices on Wednesday, 9 September 2015. The authors have greatly benefited from discussion and feedback from participants at the event. In compiling this book, we would also like to acknowledge the comments and discussion provided by Rym Ayadi, Laura Chiaramonte, Adrian Coles, Claudia Girardone, David Llewellyn, Donal McKillop, Philip Molyneux, Barry Quinn, Anna Sarkisyan, John O.S. Wilson, Robin Fieth, Chris Lawrenson, Jeremy Palmer, and Simon Rex. We also want to acknowledge the support of our home institutions, Cass Business School, City University London, and the BSA.

Finally, we wish to thank our families for their encouragement and support. Barbara Casu thanks her husband for his help with various aspects of this book and her children for their patience. Andrew Gall thanks his wife for her constant support.

Acronyms and Abbreviations

AGM	Annual General Meeting
APPG	All-Party Parliamentary Group
AT1	Additional Tier 1
ATM	Automated Teller Machine
BBA	British Bankers' Association
BCBS	Basel Committee on Banking Supervision
BOE	Bank of England
BSA	Building Societies Association
C/I	Cost-to-Income
CCDS	Core Capital Deferred Shares
CET1	Common Equity Tier 1
CRR	Capital Requirements Regulation
DBS	Dunfermline Building Society
DTI	Debt-to-Income
ECB	European Central Bank
EU	European Union
FCA	Financial Conduct Authority
FLS	Funding for Lending Scheme
FOS	Financial Ombudsman Service
FPC	Financial Policy Committee
FSA	Financial Services Authority
FSCS	Financial Services Compensation Scheme
HBOS	Halifax Bank of Scotland
ICB	Independent Commission on Banking
IFS	Institute for Fiscal Studies
IT	Information Technology
KRBS	Kent Reliance Building Society

LIBOR	London Interbank Offered Rate
LTI	Loan-to-Income
LTV	Loan-to-Value
M&S	Marks and Spencer
MBBGs	Major British Banking Groups
MPC	Monetary Policy Committee
NAB	National Australia Bank
NIM	Net Interest Margin
NS&I	National Savings & Investments
OBS	Off-Balance Sheet
ONS	Office for National Statistics
PIBS	Permanent Interest Bearing Shares
plc	Public Limited Company
PPDS	Profit Participating Deferred Shares
PPI	Payment Protection Insurance
PRA	Prudential Regulatory Authority
RBS	Royal Bank of Scotland
ROA	Return on Assets
ROE	Return on Equity
SFTs	Securities Financing Transactions
TBTF	Too-Big-To-Fail
UK	United Kingdom
UKAR	UK Asset Resolution
UKFI	UK Financial Investments Ltd
US	United States of America
YoY	Year on Year

Contents

List of Figures

List of Tables

CHAPTER 1

Financial Services and the UK Economy

Abstract The UK financial services industry is undergoing a period of deep transformation, which affects all industry participants. This chapter reviews the impact of the global financial crisis on UK banking and discusses the events that lead to unprecedented government intervention and subsequent regulatory reforms. It also provides an overview of the changing structure of the UK banking and financial sectors. While UK banking is still dominated by few very large banking groups, the recent entrance of new banks has increased its competitive nature, particularly in the retail banking sector.

1.1 Introduction

The UK banking and financial sector has been severely impacted by the events of 2007–2008, which resulted in UK banks suffering big losses forcing significant government intervention in the sector. State aid was then followed by wide-ranging regulatory reforms, aimed at making the sector more resilient to shocks, by limiting risk-taking and improving bank conduct. The main outcome of the reform process has been the Financial Services (Banking Reform) Act of December 2013, which targets bank business models, with a view to "ring-fence" retail and wholesale banking activities.

The UK banking market is dominated by the presence of large banking groups: Lloyds, HSBC, the Royal Bank of Scotland (RBS), and Barclays

B. Casu, A. Gall, *Building Societies in the Financial Services Industry*,
DOI 10.1057/978-1-137-60208-4_1

control nearly 50 % of the mortgage market, 77 % of the personal current account market, and 85 % of small business banking (Molyneux 2016).

In the post-crisis banking landscape, political efforts to increase competition in the sector have led to new entry: in 2010, Metro Bank was the first to obtain a full banking licence in over a century and since then several new banks have been authorised by regulators (British Bankers' Association 2014). These new entrants are referred to as challenger banks because they compete in a market dominated by long-established operators. Challenger banks have been remarkably successful in expanding their loan books and making some inroads in the retail market. This increased competition in the system, in addition to the effect of regulatory reforms, as well as far-reaching technological innovations, presents new challenges for the building societies sector.

Against this background, this chapter outlines the key events that impacted the UK banking market since the outbreak of the global financial crisis in 2007. Section 1.2 provides a brief outlook of the UK; Section 1.3 discusses the impact of the global financial crisis on UK banking and financial markets. Section 1.4 examines the recent regulatory developments and structural reforms. Section 1.5 presents a brief analysis of the industry structure and performance and Section 1.6 concludes the chapter.

1.2 A Brief Overview of the UK Economy

After more than a decade and a half of steady growth, the UK economy was officially declared to be in a recession in January 2009. The recession was a consequence of the credit crunch that began in the USA in August 2007 and which resulted in a global financial crisis starting in the autumn of 2008. It is now more than seven years since Lehman Brothers collapsed, ushering in the worst phase of the financial crisis, and the UK economy has been recovering at a relatively strong rate since early 2013 (Fig. 1.1).

In 2014, the UK economy grew by 3.0 %, the fastest rate since 2007 and the strongest growth rate in the G7 group of countries (Office for National Statistics). UK growth has been driven primarily by services and is projected to continue at a solid pace in 2015 and 2016, boosted by domestic demand (Institute for Fiscal Studies (IFS)). There are still, however, causes for concern. For example, while the household debt-to-income (DTI) ratio has fallen over the last three years, it remains around 150 %, significantly higher than those of other European countries and the USA.

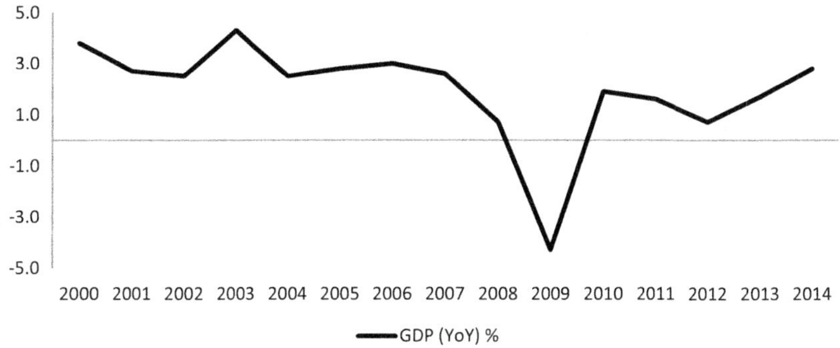

Fig. 1.1 GDP growth (%) Year on Year (*Source*: Office for National Statistics (ONS) and authors' calculations)

After several false starts following the financial crisis, the UK economy seems to be enjoying a period of sustained strong growth, helped by low oil prices, low inflation boosting purchasing power, and low interest rates fostering investment. It is expected that the low cost of finance will help maintain domestic demand growth. Rising house prices have also supported consumer confidence and spending (Fig. 1.2 and Table 1.1).

Although the UK economy is continuing to recover, the recession triggered by the global financial crisis had serious repercussion in many areas. UK banking was hit dramatically by the global financial crisis. A once profitable, innovative, and dynamic industry virtually collapsed, exposing a series of weaknesses that increased the severity of the crisis and its impact on the UK's economy.

1.3 The Global Financial Crisis and Its Impact on UK Banking

The rapid growth of the financial sector—particularly in terms of the relative size of wholesale financial services within the overall economy—accompanied by an increase in leverage (asset to capital) and an increase in the complexity of the financial system are considered some of the key causes of the crisis. In addition, the growing scale of banking activities coincided with changing forms of maturity transformation, which led to an underestimation of risk. As a leading financial centre, the UK was

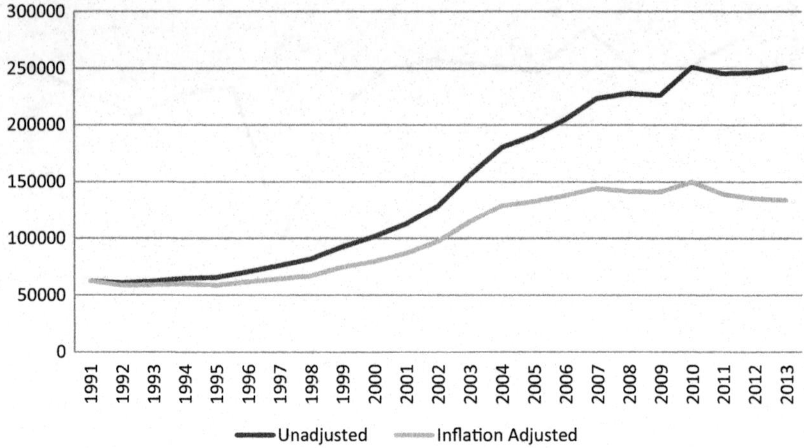

Fig. 1.2 UK average house prices (*Source*: Office for National Statistics (ONS) and authors' calculations)

greatly exposed to these factors, which played a crucial role in reinforcing the severity of the financial crisis.

The decade prior to the onset of the global financial crisis saw major changes in the way banks conduct their business, with many financial institutions extending beyond the conventional intermediation role. This entailed a change in banks' business models, which fuelled banking sector growth and risk-taking. The failure of some of these banks in the late 2000s exposed the limitations of these business models and spurred fundamental changes in regulation and supervision.

Northern Rock was the first casualty of the crisis in September 2007. The following year, Lloyds TSB announced that it was to acquire Halifax Bank of Scotland (HBOS) for £12 billion, creating a merged entity with a market share of around one-third of the UK savings and mortgage markets. In September 2008, the UK government also announced the acquisition of the mortgage-lending arm of Bradford & Bingley, and selling of the still-viable depositor base and branch network to the Spanish Santander banking group. In October 2008, capital injections were announced for RBS and Lloyds TSB and HBOS, thus increasing the government stakes in their ownership to around 60 % and 40 %, respectively. In November 2008, the UK government set up a new "arms-length" company, UK

Table 1.1 Economic Indicators

	Economic growth (YoY, %)	*Inflation (YoY, %)*			*Household income*		
	GDP	*CPI*	*RPIX*	*RPI*	*Real household disposable income (YoY, %)*	*Saving ratio (%)*	*Household debt-to-income ratio (%)*
2000	3.8	0.8	2.1	3	6.5	9.8	112
2001	2.7	1.2	2.1	1.8	4.9	10.7	119
2002	2.5	1.3	2.2	1.7	2.7	9.9	130
2003	4.3	1.4	2.8	2.9	2.7	9.2	141
2004	2.5	1.3	2.2	3	1.2	7.7	152
2005	2.8	2.1	2.3	2.8	2.1	7	154
2006	3	2.3	2.9	3.2	1.8	6.5	164
2007	2.6	2.3	3.2	4.3	2.4	7.1	168
2008	0.7	3.6	4.3	4	-0.6	5.6	167
2009	-4.3	2.2	2	-0.5	2.3	9.3	159
2010	1.9	3.3	4.8	4.6	0.9	11	151
2011	1.6	4.5	5.3	5.2	-1.9	8.6	150
2012	0.7	2.8	3.2	3.2	1.6	8	147
2013	1.7	2.6	3.1	3	-0.2	6.4	147
2014	3.0	1.5	2.4	2.4	1.5	6.0	144

Source: Office for National Statistics (ONS), Bank of England, and authors' calculations. YoY = Year on Year

Financial Investments Ltd (UKFI), to manage the banks in public ownership, Northern Rock and Bradford & Bingley. In 2013, Cheltenham & Gloucester branches and accounts were transferred to TSB, within the Lloyds Banking Group. TSB was revived, as a separate brand, after the EU demanded Lloyds Banking Group spin off 631 branches as a condition of its bailout in 2008. TSB has been sold to Spanish bank Sabadell in 2015.

A global financial crisis that caused wholesale money markets to cease functioning, undermining the confidence of retail depositors, resulting in one of the deepest recessions for many generations, including a 20 % decline in house prices, would clearly affect banks and building societies substantially. However, not all types of financial institutions followed the same path to balance sheet expansion and increased risk-taking and were therefore not affected in the same way by the crisis. In particular, the legislative constraints on building societies prevented them from adopting the business models of some of the failed banks. For example, Northern Rock sourced more than 75 % of its funding from wholesale markets, whereas societies are limited to 50 % and the average across the sector in 2007 was nearer 30 %.

Nonetheless, the building society sector was not immune to the effects of the global financial crisis of 2007–2008. Yet, in 2012 the Treasury noted:

> "Building societies survived the financial crisis in better health than the UK banking industry as a whole. This can largely be attributed to:
>
> - their low-risk focus—driven by the lending and funding limits—on residential lending and customer deposit-based funding;
> - the statutory restrictions on certain treasury activities;
> - their strong brands and higher levels of capitalisation;
> - their emphasis on longer-term planning rather than the pursuit of short term gains; and
> - their focus on serving the interests of their members, rather than meeting external shareholder pressure."

(HM Treasury, 2012)

Nevertheless, all types of banks and financial institutions are now facing the new challenges and responding to the changes in the regulatory structure.

1.4 Financial Sector Regulatory Reforms

The events of 2007–2009 also revealed the weaknesses of the existing regulatory system and set the agenda for regulatory reform. The UK authorities have introduced wide-ranging reforms. The 2012 Financial Services Act abolished the existing financial regulator, the Financial Services Authority (FSA), and created three new regulatory bodies: the Financial Policy Committee (FPC), the Prudential Regulatory Authority (PRA), and the Financial Conduct Authority (FCA). Two of the three new bodies are within the Bank of England (the FPC and the PRA, which is a subsidiary); while the FCA is a separate body responsible for business, consumer protection, and market conduct. In addition, the 2013 Banking Reform Act introduced the most significant reform of the UK banking sector in a generation, largely based on the recommendations of the Independent

Commission on Banking (ICB), which reported in September 2011 (also known as the Vickers Report). The 2013 Financial Services (Banking) Reform Act will bring into law structural and cultural changes to the banking system by (i) introducing a "ring-fence" around the deposits of people and small businesses, to separate the high street from the trading floor and protect taxpayers when things go wrong (by 2019), which will require the largest UK banks to carry out wide-reaching reorganisations of their businesses; (ii) making sure the new PRA can hold banks to account for the way they separate their retail and investment activities, giving it powers to enforce the full separation of individual banks; (iii) imposing higher standards of conduct on the banking industry by introducing a criminal sanction for reckless misconduct that leads to bank failure, the penalties for which can include an unlimited fine and a custodial sentence of up to seven years; (iv) giving depositors, protected under the Financial Services Compensation Scheme (FSCS), preference if a bank fails; (v) giving the government power to ensure that banks are more able to absorb losses; and (vi) introducing a price cap on payday loans. The provisions in the Act are due to come into force on various dates between now and 1 January 2019. These reforms are far reaching and will lead to the creation of a new financial landscape. Banking groups will be broken up into retail and wholesale/investment banking entities. These changes will affect all deposit-taking institutions, save for the smallest of them. The various reforms are therefore expected to affect both the Major British Banking Groups (MBBGs) and the building societies sector.

While the focus of the discussion so far has been on the recent regulatory reforms, it is important to recall that the current structure of the UK banking sector has been shaped by earlier reforms. To understand the ongoing changes brought on by the global financial crisis, it is necessary to step a little further back in time and discuss the changes that shaped the UK financial sector from the 1980s to the mid-2000s. A number of regulatory changes, known as the Big Bang, reduced demarcation lines between different types of financial service firms, especially between banks and building societies, as well as commercial and investment banking business. Under the 1986 Building Societies Act, building societies were given the option to convert to public limited company (plc) (and bank) status. In 1989, Abbey National was the first building society to exercise the option and convert to a bank.

Changes governing the regulatory treatment of the building society sector have had a major impact on the competitive environment in the retail banking sector. Paradoxically, reforms that were put in place to improve the competitive stance of the mutual sector vis-à-vis commercial banks led to a systematic decline of the former. This is because most of the largest building societies embraced demutualisation, leading to a shift of assets from the mutual to commercial banking sector. Some commentators have branded the demutualisation as a large failure, as the demutualised building societies have played a large part in the UK banking crisis, from the failure of Northern Rock, Bradford & Bingley, and Alliance & Leicester to the troubles of the Halifax. These banks had to be absorbed into mainstream banking groups at the height of the banking crisis and this led to a profound reorganisation of the banking sector (a detailed discussion of the demutualisation process is provided in Chapter 2).

1.5 The Structure of the UK Banking and Financial Sector

In contrast to other large European countries, the UK has a relatively small number of banks. The market is dominated by the high street banks (also known as the Major British Banking Groups—MBBGs), which include Santander UK; Barclays; HBOS, HSBC Bank; Lloyds TSB; the RBS, NatWest, and the new entrant Virgin Money (previously Northern Rock). Appendix 1.1 illustrates the composition of MBBGs over time. Other UK banks include Standard Chartered; the Co-operative Bank; Yorkshire Bank and Clydesdale Bank. The total number of authorised banking institutions has fallen from around 600 in 1985 to 313 by 2015. Of these, 155 are UK incorporated, 77 are incorporated in the European Economic Area, and 81 are incorporated outside the European Economic Area. The decline in the total number of banks is attributable to foreign banks acquiring UK banks as well as consolidation in the domestic retail banking market, following the demutualisation of building societies in the 1990s.

Up until the end of 2007, the MBBG included Abbey National, Alliance & Leicester, Barclays, Bradford & Bingley, HBOS, HSBC Bank, Lloyds TSB, Northern Rock, and the RBS. Four of these were mutual building societies that converted to bank status—Abbey National (converted in 1989), Alliance & Leicester (in 1997), Northern Rock (in 1997), and Bradford & Bingley (in 2000). HBOS was formed by the merger of Halifax (that converted into plc and bank status in June 1997) and the Bank of Scotland in September 2001. Since mid-2007, the MBBGs have experienced turmoil and there have been significant developments adversely affecting their activities.

The British Bankers' Association (BBA) (2012) has changed the definition of MBBGs to "the main high street banking groups." By 2015, the term refers to the UK activity of 21 institutions across the following banking groups: Barclays, HSBC Bank, Lloyds Banking Group, RBS Group, Santander UK, and Virgin Money.

A large-scale consolidation process has also occurred in the building society sector. There were over 2000 building societies at the beginning of the twentieth century, but today they are a movement dominated by the larger societies (a more detailed account of the history of the building societies sector is provided in Chapter 2). Figure 1.3 shows the steady decline in the number of banks and building societies, particularly in the post-crisis period.

Building societies' numbers fell from 59 in 2007 to 44 in 2014. The key merger activity included that of the Britannia Building Society with the Co-operative Bank in 2009. In the same year, the merger between Skipton and Scarborough Building Societies was completed, and in 2010 the Yorkshire Building Society and Chelsea Building Society merged, as did Coventry and Stroud and Swindon Building Societies. Notably, Nationwide acquired the troubled Dunfermline Building Society (DBS)

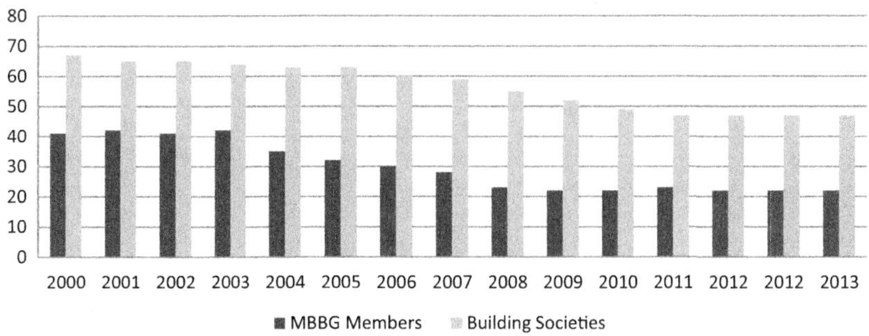

Fig. 1.3 Number of banks and building societies (2000–2013) (*Source*: Data from the British Bankers' Association (BBA) and authors' calculations. Major British Banking Groups (MBBGs) in 2000 included the following: Abbey National Group, Alliance & Leicester Group, Barclays Group, Bradford & Bingley plc (from 2000), The HBOS Group, HSBC Bank Group, Lloyds TSB Group, Northern Rock Group (from 1999), and the Royal Bank of Scotland Group. In 2013, they comprised Santander UK Group, Barclays Group, HSBC Banking Group, the Lloyds Banking Group, the Royal Bank of Scotland Group)

in 2009. The sector has seen some further consolidation, with three mergers between 2013 and 2014.[1]

Nationwide is by far the largest, with group assets over £195 billion at the end of 2014, followed by the Yorkshire Building Society, which has £37.5 billion in assets and the Coventry Building Society with assets of £31 billion (the top five societies account for over 80 % of the sector's assets).

Post crisis, a number of new contenders appeared in the industry. As discussed above, Metro Bank was the first de novo high street bank to obtain a full banking licence in over a century. By the end of 2014, Metro Bank had 31 branches (mostly around Greater London and the South East); it has grown its total number of customer accounts from 8,912 in 2010 to 447,000 in 2014. Since April 2013, the PRA has granted 11 new banking licenses. Many of these are overseas entrants, with a greater focus on treasury or capital market operations. However, there are also the next wave of challenger banks: OakNorth, Atom, Starling, and CivilisedBank (KPMG 2015) (Fig. 1.4).

The global financial crisis has also had a negative impact on UK banking sector employment: the main UK banks have shed around 25,000 staff since mid-2007 and this puts total employment down from 318,300 to 292,600 by 2012. The average staff costs accounted for 0.6 % of total

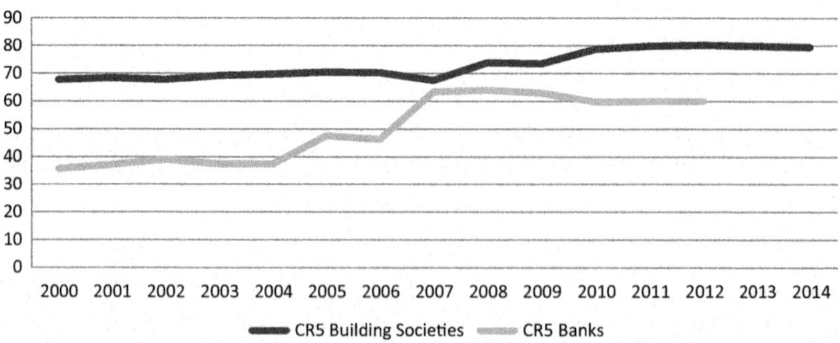

Fig. 1.4 Concentration ratio (CR5) (*Source*: SNL; Building Societies Association (BSA) and authors' calculations. Note the Building Societies CR5 is calculated as the sum of total assets of the five largest building societies over the total building society sector's assets; the CR5 for banks is calculated as the sum of the five largest banks over the total banking sector's assets)

assets and remained at a stable proportion for the period 2009–2012 (British Bankers' Association 2013).

The largest employer in 2012 was Lloyds Banking Group (110,295 employees, of which 96,600 in the UK), followed by HSBC Bank (74,190 employees, of which 43,800 in the UK). The RBS was the largest employer in 2007 with 203,500 but only had 71,200 by the end of 2012. The building society sector followed a similar trend, the total number of staff employed decreased from 48,944 in 2007 to 39,397 in 2012 (although there are signs of the trend reversing in recent years, as the total number of staff employed increased by almost a 1,000–40,220 by the end of 2014). The largest employer was Nationwide, which almost doubled the number of staff employed between 2000 and 2007 (from 9,741 to 16,815 in 2007), and continued to increase its workforce (it had 17,268 by the end of 2014). Table 1.2 highlights the trends in employment in the UK banking and building societies sector between 2000 and 2012. Notably, while the largest banking groups underwent major restructuring, the largest building societies have displayed steady growth rates over the period. This trend is confirmed when considering the proportion of employment in banks and building societies, as percentage of total employment (see Fig. 1.5).

Notwithstanding the forced impact of the financial crisis, UK banks and building societies have engaged in significant reorganisation over the past 15 years. This is characterised by the decline in branch numbers, a trend that further accelerated post crisis, with a fall from 10,051 in 2006 to 8,837 in 2012 (British Bankers' Association 2013).

Figure 1.6 shows the trends in branch and Automated Teller Machine (ATM) numbers in the UK since 1990 and illustrates that during the 1990s, while branch numbers were declining, the number of ATMs grew significantly. The reason for the shift from branches to other means of financial service delivery mainly relates to UK retail financial service firms' desire to improve operating efficiency as well as customers' increasing demands to access banking services outside traditional (rather limited) banking hours. The number of ATMs at bank branches has increased substantially as banks have been automating not only cash withdrawal functions but also pay-in services (often dramatically reducing the number of cashiers). ATMs have also increased in remote locations, such as in retail outlets. The decrease in branch numbers has been a trend even in the building society sector, although the reduction has not been as marked: branch numbers fell from 2,139 in 2000 to 1,943 in 2007 to just over 1,600 by the end of 2014.

Table 1.2 Total Staff—Banks and Building Societies (2000–2012)

			2000	*2007*	*2012*
MBBGs					
	Santander		n/a	n/a	25,800
		Abbey National	19,400	14,100	n/a
		Alliance & Leicester	9200	8100	
	Barclays		56,500	58,300	49,600
		Woolwich	7,700	n/a	n/a
	Bradford & Bingley		7,700	3100	n/a
	HBOS		n/a	74,087	n/a
		Halifax	26,100	n/a	n/a
		Bank of Scotland	12,800	n/a	n/a
	HSBC Bank		48,000	49,500	43,800
	Lloyds Banking Group		n/a	n/a	96,600
	Lloyds TSB		n/a	50,600	
		Lloyds	57,400	n/a	n/a
		TSB Group	n/a	n/a	n/a
	The Royal Bank of Scotland		19,700	80,400	74,200
		National Westminster	47,500	n/a	n/a
	Northern Rock		3,100	6700	n/a
	Virgin Money		n/a	n/a	2,600
Total MBBGs			**307,300**	**318,300**	**292,600**
Other banks					
	Bristol & West		2,800	n/a	n/a
	Clydesdale Bank		3,600	8,850	10,400
	Yorkshire Bank		4,900	1,789	1,896
	The Co-operative Bank		4,000	4,300	7,400

(*continued*)

Table 1.2 (continued)

		2000	*2007*	*2012*
Building societies	Nationwide	12,908	16,815	17,706
	Britannia	3,322	5,014	n/a
	Yorkshire	1,852	2,364	4,088
	Coventry	960	1282	1847
	Skipton	2,966	9,977	8,438
	Leeds	840	987	946
	Principality	588	1,206	1,242
Total building societies		**34,774**	**48,955**	**39,397**

Source: British Bankers' Association (BBA); Building Societies Association (BSA) and authors' calculations. Note these figures exclude staff working outside the UK.

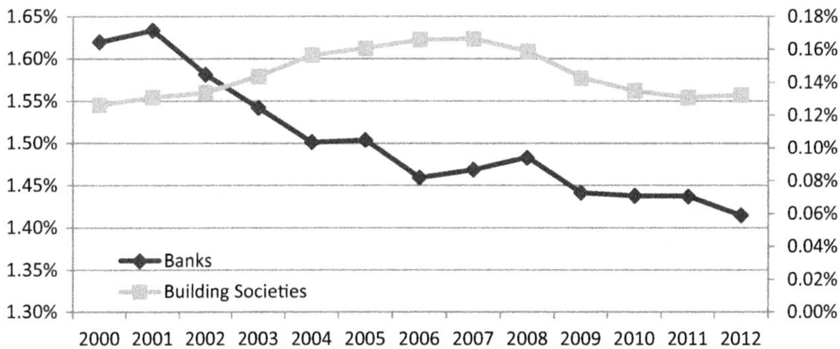

Fig. 1.5 Total employment in banks and building societies (as % of total employment) (*Source*: British Bankers' Association (BBA); Building Societies Association (BSA); Office for National Statistics (ONS) and authors' calculations)

In recent years, banks and building societies have been under pressure to re-think their distribution networks, with a view to cut costs, which resulted in the aforementioned decrease in both staff and branch numbers. Banks and building societies have been increasingly competing in the retail mortgage market, where they faced competition also from specialised lenders and, in more recent years, from challenger banks.

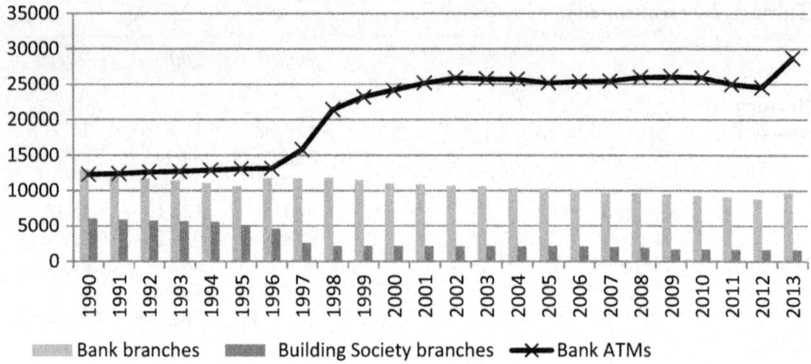

Fig. 1.6 Branches and ATMs (1990–2013) (*Source*: British Bankers' Association (BBA) and authors' calculations)

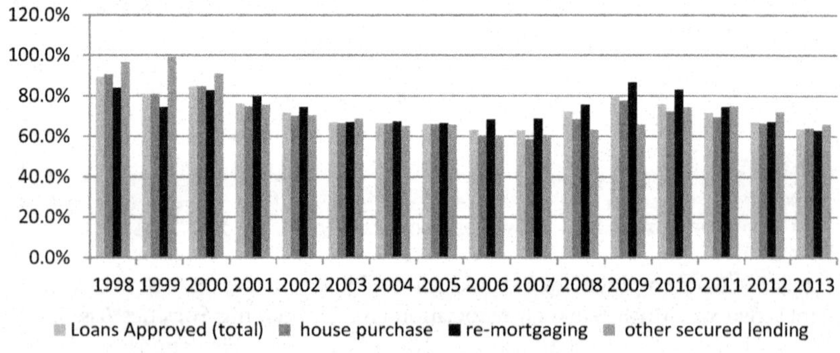

Fig. 1.7 High street banks' share of new lending approvals (%) (*Source:* British Bankers' Association (BBA) and authors' calculations. High street banks were previously named MBBGs—Major British Banking Groups)

The "big five" (HSBC, Barclays, Lloyds, RBS, and Santander) together still have the largest share of new lending approvals (see Fig. 1.7). However, the so-called Large Challengers also have substantial market share. Among the latter are Virgin Money, The Post Office, and William & Glyns; in addition, the new TSB, the National Australia Bank (NAB), and the building society Nationwide.

In addition, the major retailers such as Marks & Spencer (M&S), Asda Money, Tesco, and Sainsbury's all are developing their retail banking services via online and store offerings. The longer established ones, Tesco and M&S (provided by HSBC), are expanding their offering with products such as current accounts and mortgages thus further challenging the big banks (KPMG 2015).

Despite the undeniable impact of the global financial crisis, the UK banking landscape presents both challenges and opportunities. High street banks are still dealing with major restructuring operations and cost-cutting. However, UK banking seems now in a better shape than in the pre-crisis years, attracting new entrants which have increased the competition dynamics and are forcing banks to re-think their distribution networks as well as their product offering.

1.6 Conclusion

Although the UK economy is continuing to recover, the recession triggered by the global financial crisis had serious repercussion in many areas. UK banking was severely hit by the global financial crisis. As a consequence, UK regulators have introduced extensive reforms aimed at making the banking sector safer and more resilient. These reforms seem to have been successful in strengthening banks' capital positions in excess of the minimum regulatory requirements and the sector seems to have returned to some profitability. Nonetheless, the operating environment continues to be challenging and the new regulations impose increased burdens on financial institutions' balance sheets. However, as the economic situation is improving, the outlook for the sector is positive.

1.7 Appendix 1.1 Major British Banking Groups (MBBGs)

Year	*Banking Group Name*	*Subsidiaries*
1985–1996	The Standard Chartered Group	Chartered Trust plc Chartered WestLB Ltd Standard Chartered Bank
1985–1994	The TSB Group	Hill Samuel Bank Ltd (from 1987) TSB Bank plc TSB Bank Northern Ireland plc (up to 1991) TSB Bank Scotland plc United Dominions Trust
Until 1994	The Lloyds Group	Lloyds Bowmaker Ltd Cedar Holdings Ltd (form 1981 to 1988) Lloyds Bank plc Lloyds Bank (LABCO) Ltd (up to 1986) Lloyds Bank International Ltd (merged into Lloyds Bank plc in 1986) Lloyds Bank Finance (Jersey) Ltd (up to 1992) Lloyds Private Banking Ltd (from 1992) LMB Services Ltd (from 1985 up to 1993) The National Bank of New Zealand Ltd (up to 1991)
1995–2008	The Lloyds TSB Group	AMC Bank Ltd Black Horse Ltd (2001 & 2002 only) Cheltenham & Gloucester plc Hill Samuel Bank Ltd (up to 1998) Lloyds Bank (BLSA) Ltd (from 1998 to 2002) Lloyds TSB Bank plc Lloyds TSB Private Banking Ltd Lloyds TSB Scotland plc Lloyds UDT Ltd (up to 2002) Scottish Widows Bank plc (from 2000) TSB Bank plc (up to and including 1998 when it merged with Lloyds Bank) United Dominions Trust Ltd (1997 only)

(*continued*)

Year	*Banking Group Name*	*Subsidiaries*
From 2009	The Lloyds Banking Group	Halifax plc Bank of Scotland (from 2009) HBOS Treasury Services plc (up to 2006) Capital Bank plc (up to 2006) Lloyds TSB Bank plc (from 2009) AMC Bank Ltd (from 2009) Cheltenham & Gloucester plc Lloyds TSB Private Banking Ltd (from 2009) Lloyds TSB Scotland plc (from 2009) Scottish Widows Bank plc (from 2009)
Until 2008	Alliance & Leicester Group	Alliance & Leicester plc Alliance & Leicester Commercial Bank plc (from 2003 to 2006) Alliance & Leicester Group Treasury plc (up to 2001)
2000–2009	Bradford & Bingley plc	Bradford & Bingley failed in 2008 and was partly transferred into public ownership. In 2010, it was integrated into a new holding company, UK Asset Resolution (UKAR)
1999–2008	Northern Rock Group	Legal & General Bank Ltd (2002 only) Northern Rock plc
Until 1999	The National Westminster Group	County NatWest Ltd (up to 1994) Coutts & Co Coutts Finance Co (up to 1989) Gartmore Money Management Ltd (from 1996) International Westminster Bank plc (merged into National Westminster Bank PMV in 1989) Isle of Man Bank (up to 1981) Lombard Bank (Isle of Man) (up to 1992) Lombard Bank Ltd (from 1987) Lombard Banking (Jersey) (up to 1992) Lombard North Central plc Lombard & Ulster Ltd (from 1985) National Westminster Bank plc National Westminster Bank Finance (C.I.) Ltd (up to 1989) Ulster Bank Ltd (from 1985) Ulster Bank Trust Company (from 1987 to 1990) Ulster Investment Bank Ltd (from 1985)

(*continued*)

Year	*Banking Group Name*	*Subsidiaries*
2015	The Royal Bank of Scotland Group	Adam and Company plc (from 1993) Charterhouse Bank Ltd (from 1985 to 1993) Charterhouse Japhet plc (1986 and 1987 only) Coutts & Co (from 2000) Cripps Warburg Ltd (up to 1981) Direct Line Financial Services (up to 2006) GEM Money Management Ltd (up to 2002) Lombard Bank Ltd (from 2000 to 2005) Lombard North Central plc (from 2000 to 2003) Lombard & Ulster Ltd (from 2000) National Commercial & Glyn's Ltd (up to 1986) National Westminster Bank plc (from 2000) RBS Trust Bank Ltd (up to 1998) Royal Bank of Scotland NV (from 2011) RoyScot Trust plc (from 1981 to 2002) Tesco Personal Finance Ltd (from 1998) The Royal Bank of Scotland plc Ulster Bank Ltd (from 2000) Ulster Bank Ireland Ltd (from 2000) Williams & Glyn's plc (merged into The Royal Bank of Scotland plc in 1985) Williams & Glyn's Bank Investments (Jersey) (up 1981) Williams & Glyn's Bank Investments (Guernsey) (up to 1981) Williams & Glyn's Bank Investments (Isle of Man) (up to 1981)
1991–2008	The Abbey National Group (acquired by Santander in 2004)	Abbey National plc (including retail deposits of Bradford & Bingley from 2008) Abbey National Treasury Services plc CA Premier Banking (from 2001 to 2005) Cater Allen (from 1997) First National Bank plc (from 1995) First National Commercial Bank plc (from 1995 up to and including 1997)

(*continued*)

Year	*Banking Group Name*	*Subsidiaries*
From 2009	Santander UK Group	Santander UK (including retail deposits of Bradford & Bingley from 2008) Abbey National Treasury Services plc CA Premier Banking (up to 2005) Cater Allen Alliance & Leicester plc (from 2008) Alliance & Leicester Commercial Bank plc (from 2003 to 2006)
1997–2000	Halifax plc	
Until 2000	The Bank of Scotland Group	Bank of Scotland Bank of Scotland Treasury Services plc (from 1992) Bank of Wales plc (from 1986 up to 2001) Capital Bank (formerly NWS Bank plc) (from 1981) The British Linen Bank Ltd
2001–2008	The HBOS Group	Bank of Scotland Bank of Wales plc (up to 2000) Capital Bank plc (up to 2006) Halifax plc (up to 2006) HBOS Treasury Services plc (up to 2006) The British Linen Bank Ltd (up to 2000)
2015	The Barclays Group	Barclays Bank plc Barclays Bank International Ltd (merged into Barclays Bank plc in 1985) Barclays Bank Finance Company (Jersey) Ltd (up to 1996) Barclays Bank Trust Company Ltd Barclays Capital Finance Ltd (up to 1997) Barclays de Zoete Wedd Ltd (up to 1998) Barclays Finance Company (Guernsey) Ltd (up to 1996) Barclays Finance Company (Isle of Man) Ltd (up to 1996) Barclays Private Bank Ltd (from 1996 to 2006) Mercantile Credit Company Ltd (up to 1991) Woolwich plc (from 1997 to 2003)

(*continued*)

Year	*Banking Group Name*	*Subsidiaries*
2015	The HSBC Bank Group (formerly Midland Group)	Clydesdale Bank Finance Corporation Ltd (from 1985 to 1987) Clydesdale Bank plc (up to 1987) Crocker National Bank (from 1981 to 1986) Forward Trust Group (up to 1998) Forward Trust Personal Finance (from 1987 to and 1995) HSBC Asset Finance (UK) Ltd (up to 1999) HSBC Bank plc (formerly Midland Bank plc) HSBC Trust Company (UK) Ltd (formerly Midland Bank Trust Company Ltd) (from 1987) Marks & Spencer Financial Services (from 2011) Northern Bank Development Corporation Ltd (from 1985 to 1987) Northern Bank Ltd (from 1985 to 1987) Midland Bank Trust Corporation (Guernsey) Ltd (up to 1991) Midland Bank Trust Corporation (Jersey) Ltd (up to 1991) Midland Bank Trust Corporation (Isle of Man) Ltd (up to 1991) Samuel Montagu & Co Ltd (up to 1993) Samuel Montagu & Co (Jersey) Ltd (merged with Midland Bank Trust Company (Jersey) Ltd in 1988) Samuel Montagu (MFBC) Ltd (up to and including 1977)

Source: British Bankers' Association—Abstract of Banking Statistics, various years

Notes

1. On the 1 February 2013, Century Building Society merged with Scottish Building Society. On the 1 July 2013, Shepshed Building Society merged with Nottingham Building Society. On the 1 July 2014, City of Derry Building Society merged with Progressive Building Society.

References

British Bankers' Association. (2012). Banking business. *An Abstract of Banking Statistics, 29.*

British Bankers' Association (2014) Banking Business. An Abstract of Banking Statistics, volume 31.

British Bankers' Association. (2013). Banking business. *An Abstract of Banking Statistics, 30.*

HM Treasury. (2012). The future of building societies. HM Treasury, July. Available at https://www.gov.uk/government/uploads/system/uploads/attachment_data/file/81426/condoc_future_building_societies.pdf

KPMG (2015) Building Societies Database, available at https://assets.kpmg.com/content/dam/kpmg/pdf/2016/01/building-societies-database-2015.pdf.

Molyneux P. (2016) Banking in the UK in Beck T. and Casu B. (eds.) The Handbook of European Banking, Chapter 20, Palgrave McMillan.

CHAPTER 2

A Brief History of Building Societies

Abstract This chapter begins by recounting some of the main points in the building society sector's development, then adds to the historical account by describing some of the more recent changes to arrive at the shape we have today. We focus in particular on the demutualisation process that saw the largest building societies becoming banks. We then assess the impact of the financial crisis on the sector; we analyse the consolidation process that took place as larger and more sound building societies took over troubled ones. The sector required little direct government support during the crisis, with the exception of the failure of the Dunfermline Building Society (DBS) in 2009.

2.1 Introduction to Building Societies

Building societies are specialist financial institutions that are owned by their customers. This ownership structure has had a profound impact on how they are run since the first societies were founded almost 250 years ago. The origins of building societies have been described in detail in several previous studies (Cleary 1965; Boleat 1981). However, this history remains relevant to the building societies operating today as it informs their ethos, and some still operate with their original charters in place.

This is not to say that building societies are an historical artefact. No sector that survives for 250 years can stay fixed to its original structures and constitution. Indeed, one of the previous surveys of the sector noted how over two centuries "building societies have been faced with a wide variety

B. Casu, A. Gall, *Building Societies in the Financial Services Industry*,
DOI 10.1057/978-1-137-60208-4_2

of economic and political environments and have succeeded in adapting themselves to these changes with considerable skill" (Cleary 1965).

Since that comment was made, the sector has undergone an abrupt transformation with ten organisations that made up the majority of the sector (by total assets) changing their form and converting to banks. This process has had a significant impact on the subsequent behaviour of many of the building societies that remained, as they re-established their focus on creating value for members. The financial crisis demonstrated that mistakes can still be made, by building societies as well as by banks, in the choice of strategy or the management of its implementation, but as we emerge from the crisis many bank competitors claim to be shaping their organisations to put customers first—a strategy that imitates one of the distinctive features of the mutual model.

2.2 Origins and Growth of a Movement

The first known building society was formed in 1775, in a public house in Birmingham. Brought together by a principle of self-help, the members of these early building societies pooled their regular savings to buy land and fund the construction of a property. They would draw lots to determine which member got the house and the process would then repeat until all the members were housed, whereupon the society would close. Hence, the first societies were called *terminating societies.* New building societies started up across the country, and by 1825 there were over 250 societies in existence.

In 1845 the first known *permanent society* was formed. It was permanent because it accepted savings from members who were not necessarily potential homeowners, enabling savers and borrowers to join and to leave membership without the society closing. By the end of 1900 there were 2,286 societies, though this was a reduction on the preceding decade when there were estimated to be over 3,600. The numbers fell rapidly, partly because of the consolidation of smaller societies, but largely as terminating societies wound up.

Table 2.1 presents some operational statistics, starting from the 1900s. Note that some of the large year-on-year changes are due to the demutualisation of large building societies, as described in Table 2.2 later in this chapter.

In 1836, the first legislation dealing specifically with building societies was introduced and in 1874 the first Building Societies Act was passed

Table 2.1 Building society operational statistics

Year	*Number of authorised societies*	*Number of branches*	*Number of investors (000s)*	*Number of depositors (000s)*	*Number of borrowers (000s)*	*Deposits from shares (£m)*	*Deposit and loan balances (£m)*	*Mortgage assets (£m)*	*Total assets (£m)*	*Amount advanced (£m)*
1900	2,286	—	585	—	—	—	—	46	60	9
1910	1,723	—	626	—	—	—	—	60	76	9
1920	1,271	—	748	—	—	64	19	69	87	25
1930	1,026	—	1,449	428	720	303	45	316	371	89
1940	952	—	2,088	771	1,503	552	142	678	756	21
1950	819	—	2,256	654	1,508	962	205	1,060	1,256	270
1960	726	—	3,910	571	2,349	2,721	222	2,647	3,166	560
1970	481	2,016	10,265	618	3,655	9,788	382	8,752	10,819	1,954
1980	273	5,684	30,636	915	5,383	48,915	1,762	42,437	53,793	9,503
1990	101	6,051	36,948	4,299	6,724	160,538	40,695	175,745	216,848	43,081
2000	67	2,361	22,237	740	3,107	119,299	43,579	134,100	177,747	31,514
2001	65	2,126	20,310	568	2,750	119,815	37,985	128,322	171,375	31,845
2002	65	2,103	20,724	511	2,688	132,373	37,651	138,884	184,453	37,303
2003	63	2,081	20,897	520	2,679	142,457	49,204	156,396	207,735	49,628
2004	63	2,074	20,734	525	2,749	153,844	63,798	180,172	236,146	59,283
2005	63	2,148	22,090	449	2,822	171,935	71,704	203,260	265,226	59,011
2006	60	2,105	22,396	472	2,857	188,943	82,760	228,096	294,419	64,564
2007	59	2,016	23,038	460	2,941	206,783	98,365	257,810	330,272	67,368
2008	55	1,916	24,990	n/a	2,926	230,879	104,302	265,554	358,956	44,772
2009	52	1,685	n/a	n/a	2,714	222,271	83,360	243,638	331,274	21,715
2010	49	1,672	c. 20,000	n/a	c. 2569	210,760	73,509	238,698	309,451	25,779
2011	47	c. 1652	c. 20,500	n/a	c. 2800	215,016	68,901	238,607	308,143	32,315
2012	47	c. 1546	c. 19,320	n/a	c. 3116	221,415	72,834	252,041	319,803	38,928

(*continued*)

Table 2.1 (continued)

Year	*Number of authorised societies*	*Number of branches*	*Number of investors (000s)*	*Number of depositors (000s)*	*Number of borrowers (000s)*	*Deposits from shares (£m)*	*Deposit and loan balances (£m)*	*Mortgage assets (£m)*	*Total assets (£m)*	*Amount advanced (£m)*
2013	45	c. 1,548	c. 19,213	n/a	c. 3,149	222,795	69,428	258,362	317,322	50,423
2014	44	c. 1,563	c. 21,098	n/a	c. 3,499	234,433	67,770	265,417	331,422	52,654

Source: Building Societies Association Yearbooks. *Note*: Years are societies' financial years ending between 1 February to 31 January in the following year; societies do not all have the same year end. The figures are based on the annual returns provided by all building societies in Great Britain. From 1986 figures include societies based in Northern Ireland. Prior to 1989 the figures for the number of societies are the number registered. From 1989 onwards the figures are the number of societies authorised to accept funds from the public (i.e. inactive societies still on the register were excluded). Before 1930 borrowers who were not shareholders were included in the number of shareholders. The number of advances includes further advances and therefore does not indicate the number of borrowers. Figures from 1993 onwards are on a group basis. Prior years are on a society-only basis

Table 2.2 Demutualisation of the UK building society sector (1989–2000)

Year	*Building society name*	*% of 1988 building society sector assets (Total: 75%)[a]*	*Nature of conversion or acquisition and where they are now (2015)*	*Years as independent company post demutualisation (until takeover/ nationalisation)*
1989	**Abbey National**	17%	Converted to plc and bank status in July 1989. Acquired by Santander in November 2004. Rebranded to **Santander** in January 2010	15
1995	**Cheltenham & Gloucester**	4%	Acquired by Lloyds TSB in August 1995. In 2013 Cheltenham & Gloucester branches and accounts were transferred to TSB, within the Lloyds Banking Group. TSB was revived, as a separate brand after the EU demanded Lloyds Banking Group spin off 631 branches as a condition of its £20bn bailout by taxpayers in 2008. TSB has been sold to Spanish bank **Sabadell** in 2015	0
1996	**National & Provincial**	4%	Acquired by Abbey National in August 1996, so now part of **Santander** group	0

(*continued*)

Table 2.2 (continued)

Year	*Building society name*	*% of 1988 building society sector assets (Total: 75 %)*[a]	*Nature of conversion or acquisition and where they are now (2015)*	*Years as independent company post demutualisation (until takeover/ nationalisation)*
1997	**Alliance & Leicester**	6%	Converted to plc and bank status in April 1997. Acquired by Santander in 2008 and rebranded as **Santander** in 2010	11
1997	**Halifax**	27%	Halifax and Leeds Permanent Building Societies merged in 1995; the new Halifax then converted into plc and bank status in June 1997. Halifax merged with the Bank of Scotland in September 2001 to form HBOS. In 2008 Lloyds Bank agreed to take over HBOS, which became part of the **Lloyds Banking Group** in 2009	4 to form HBOS, 11 until takeover by Lloyds Banking Group
1997	**Woolwich**	8%	Converted to a bank in July 1997 and acquired by **Barclays** in October 2000	3

(*continued*)

Table 2.2 (continued)

Year	*Building society name*	*% of 1988 building society sector assets (Total: 75 %)*[a]	*Nature of conversion or acquisition and where they are now (2015)*	*Years as independent company post demutualisation (until takeover/ nationalisation)*
1997	**Bristol & West**	2%	Acquired by the **Bank of Ireland** in July 1997. Bristol & West transferred its branch network and savings accounts to Britannia Building Society in 2005. This was the first remutualisation of a converted institution. Britannia became part of the Co-op Banking Group in 2009, the first merger between a building society and a mutual bank made possible under the 2007 "Butterfill Act." It is currently (2015) being rebranded to **Co-operative Bank**	0

(*continued*)

Table 2.2 (continued)

Year	*Building society name*	*% of 1988 building society sector assets (Total: 75%)[a]*	*Nature of conversion or acquisition and where they are now (2015)*	*Years as independent company post demutualisation (until takeover/ nationalisation)*
1997	**Northern Rock**	2%	Converted to bank status in October 1997. Northern Rock failed in 2008 and was transferred into **public ownership**. In 2010 was split into two entities, Northern Rock plc and Northern Rock Asset Management. In 2011 Northern Rock plc was sold to Virgin Money, which rebranded all Northern Rock branches in 2012. Northern Rock Asset Management was integrated into a new holding company, **UK Asset Resolution** (UKAR)	11
1999	**Birmingham Midshires**	1%	Acquired by Halifax in April 1999. The Halifax merged with the Bank of Scotland in September 2001 to form HBOS. Birmingham Midshires Building Society is now part of **Lloyds Banking Group**, as a division of the Bank of Scotland	0

(*continued*)

Table 2.2 (continued)

Year	*Building society name*	*% of 1988 building society sector assets (Total: 75%)*[a]	*Nature of conversion or acquisition and where they are now (2015)*	*Years as independent company post demutualisation (until takeover/ nationalisation)*
2000	**Bradford & Bingley**	4%	Converted to bank status in December 2000. Bradford & Bingley failed in 2008 upon which Santander acquired its branches and savings business, and its mortgages transferred to public ownership. In 2010 it was integrated into a new holding company, **UK Asset Resolution** (UKAR)	8

[a]Proportion of sector assets includes other societies that merged after 1988 but prior to demutualisation

into legislation. This arose out of the 1870 Royal Commission on Friendly Societies, which had also included building societies in its enquiries. The 1874 Act was then followed by other Acts, which made various amendments mainly aimed to prevent some of the more dubious or even fraudulent behaviour that had emerged at some societies. Additions were made to building society legislation through the twentieth century to tighten requirements on building societies' business, including on mortgage security and liquidity.

The Building Societies Association (BSA) started out in 1869 as The Building Societies Protection Association to act as the national body for the industry, and was renamed in 1926. In 1939 the governing Council of the Association, constituted of Chief Executives of the major building societies, started to recommend interest rates to be offered to investors and borrowers, a system which worked smoothly for several decades, effectively forming a cartel and restricting price competition between societies.

Building societies grew in size and importance in the second half of the twentieth century, and started to attract more scrutiny from the government, including on the recommended rates system. However, in the 1970s the cartel's effect in keeping variable mortgage rates low and stable was politically advantageous, and the BSA's interest rate recommendations were exempted from restrictive practices legislation.

Building societies came to dominate the mortgage market with a share of 70–80% of mortgage loans, which lasted up until the mid-1980s (see Fig. 2.1). Most societies adhered to the BSA Council's recommended rates regardless of the implications for their financial performance. Furthermore, societies signed up to give the BSA 28 days' notice of any intention to make either their mortgage or savings rates more competitive (Coles 2013). The BSA then notified all of its other member societies of the individual building society's intended rate change.

This effective cartel resulted in relatively stable interest rates, in an attempt to balance the interests of savers and borrowers on variable interest

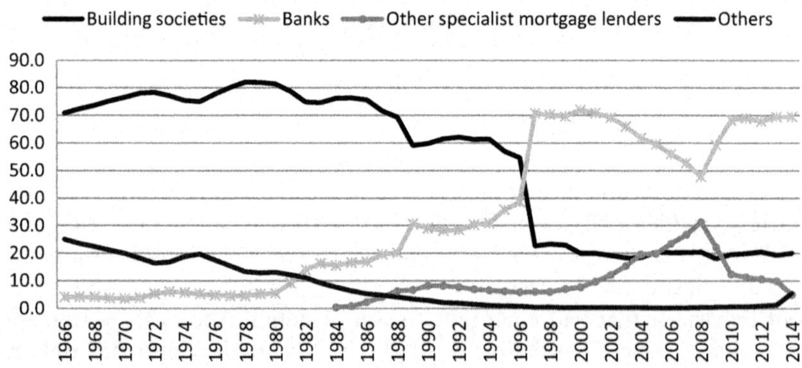

Fig. 2.1 Historic mortgage market shares (%) (*Source*: Data from BSA, Compendium of Housing Statistics, Bank of England, Authors' calculations). (*Note*: "Others" includes public sector and local authority, Pension Funds, and insurance companies. The increase in 2014 reflects a reclassification from Other Specialist Lenders. "Other specialist lenders" includes the lending subsidiaries and Special Purpose Vehicles of banks, many of which were taken back on to banks' books in the wake of the financial crisis. Building society lending subsidiaries are included in the building society series from 2005 onwards.)

rates. As a result, there was little price competition and recommended rates were often set below market clearing levels, sometimes due to political pressure. The result was frequent rationing of credit, with potential borrowers having to queue for mortgages.

Another consequence of the lack of price competition between societies was competition in non-price factors such as service standards, advertising, and branding. One of the most obvious ways of competing for customers was the proliferation of branches, with the number of building society branches more than tripling from 2,016 in 1970 to 6,480 by 1982, outstripping the increase in the number of loans approved each year by societies, which doubled over this period.

2.3 Price Competition and Demutualisation

Prior to the early 1980s, banks' ability to enter the mortgage market had been constrained by an informal agreement not to compete in this area, as well as the supplementary special deposits scheme, also known as the "corset" that applied at various times over the 1970s. This was intended to restrict the growth of the money supply by directly controlling the Sterling operations of banks. It was abolished in 1980 when banks circumvented the controls by transferring activity abroad. Freed from this constraint, banks entered the mortgage market and also began to compete for retail savings. Banks' share of mortgage balances grew from just over 5% in 1980 to over 15% in 1984, and continued to grow in subsequent years (see Fig. 2.1).

The onset of price competition led to the building society cartel breaking down. Banks were not bound by the recommendations, and some larger building societies within the cartel wanted more freedom to set rates. In 1983, Abbey National announced it would withdraw from the cartel. The BSA moved to a system of suggested rates, but this arrangement too soon broke down as competition became established.

As building societies competed with banks, the differences in their regulatory and legal positions became more relevant and in 1986 building society legislation was completely reformed. The Building Societies Act 1986 gave societies wider powers in housing and personal banking services, and allowed them to diversify into other areas such as estate agency and insurance. Building societies had recently started making greater use of wholesale funding (the first issues of Certificates of Deposit were made by societies in 1983) which was addressed with a new limit, and the conversion of a building society into a public limited company was permitted.

Starting with Abbey National in 1989, through to Bradford & Bingley in 2000, ten building societies converted to plc status, comprising 75% of the sector by 1988 assets (see Table 2.2). There was a pause after the first demutualisation due to the housing market crash and recession in the early 1990s. However, access to individual members' claims on accumulated reserves via considerable "windfall" payments upon conversion led to a rush of people—so-called carpetbaggers—queuing to open accounts in the hope of forcing or at least benefiting from a demutualisation. The boards of directors at societies that demutualised supported the conversion to plc status, though at Bradford & Bingley the board did not initially support the conversion.

Building societies that were committed to mutuality began to promote the merits as they saw them of remaining mutual, and also introduced charitable assignment clauses to reduce the incentive for carpetbaggers to become a member at a society and try to force conversion. Under these clauses, new members would agree that any windfall payments, at least for some initial period of membership, would be paid away to charity on conversion.

For several years many societies whose boards believed it was in their members' interest to retain their mutual status received resolutions at Annual General Meetings (AGM) for the board to consider conversion or merger, or to elect a known carpetbagger onto the board. Though members often voted in favour of the board considering conversion, the boards would later announce that their consideration had resulted in a decision to remain mutual. On just three occasions were conversions put to the member vote and rejected, with the BSA and affected societies working closely together to mount a defence. Nationwide's members twice rejected resolutions to convert in 1997 and 1998, and Leek United successfully defended its mutual status against a hostile takeover by Murray Financial Corporation in 1999. Murray Financial had been established with the aim of simultaneously demutualising and acquiring building societies.

In the new millennium, the former building societies, now unconstrained as plc banks, grew their lending aggressively. Halifax became part of Halifax Bank of Scotland (HBOS) plc and grew its commercial lending rapidly. Some, such as Bradford & Bingley plc, entered buy-to-let while others such as Alliance & Leicester bought mortgage books from new entrants to the mortgage market such as the American firm

GMAC. Northern Rock famously grew rapidly on a model of a low-cost base and short-term wholesale funding.

Many of these institutions were therefore extremely exposed when financial markets seized up in 2007 and the shockwaves reverberated through 2008. Northern Rock experienced a run in late 2007 and was taken into state ownership in early 2008. HBOS was merged into Lloyds TSB, and the expanded Lloyds Banking Group needed direct government support in 2009. It is now widely recognised that of the ten building societies that demutualised, none remains as an independent entity. All were either taken over by or merged with another banking group, or failed because of the financial crisis and had to be taken into public ownership. Abbey National lasted the longest on its own, at 15 years, before it was bought by Spain's Santander Group (Table 2.2).

Some of the stated aims of converting to a plc were a desire to be freed from the restrictions of building society legislation, to offer a wider range of services, and access to wholesale markets. Converting also provided the ability to raise external capital. Other potential reasons were financial gains for directors of the converting societies, or managerial hubris derived from leading a bigger, more wide-ranging bank. One study looking at data on Chief Executive remuneration at building societies before and after conversion from 1993 to 2000 found that there were large increases (greater than 300% after demutualisation) in board remuneration at demutualised societies and that these were much greater than increases in remuneration at continuing building societies. These increases could not be justified by improvements in standard company performance measures (Shiwakoti 2005). A 2006 study by the All-Party Parliamentary Group (APPG) for Building Societies and Financial Mutuals into demutualisations concluded that the benefits were questionable (APPG 2006). Whatever the actual reasons for converting, the problems subsequently faced by many of the banks prompted Vince Cable, Secretary of State for Business, Innovation, and Skills in the coalition government (2010–2015) to later describe the demutualisation episode as "one of the great acts of economic vandalism in modern times" (Cable 2012).

An important impact of the change in structure has been a less diverse financial services market. Various studies have noted the importance of diversity in terms of adding to financial stability and the effectiveness of competition (Haldane and May 2011; Ayadi et al. 2010a, b). A study by Michie and Oughton attempts to measure the change in diversity across four dimensions: the size of firms, ownership, funding model, and geographic spread (Michie and Oughton 2013). They combine these dimensions in one Diversity Index (D-Index) and find a significant decline in their indicator since 2000.

Using Michie and Oughton's approach for ownership diversity, we estimate a Corporate Diversity Index for the UK mortgage market. The index can be defined as follows:

$$CD_m = 1 - \sum_{1}^{z} \mu_j^2 \tag{2.1}$$

where $j = 1,...Z$ indicates the number of distinct corporate forms and μ represents the market share of mortgages held by banks and mutuals.

Figure 2.2 illustrates the trend in the Corporate Diversity Index. One can see that the UK mortgage market has undergone shifts in relative ownership diversity, with the demutualisations causing the most abrupt changes. There were some swings in diversity as the public sector withdrew from lending in the 1960s and early 1970s. In the decade 1970s–1980s, the dominance of mutual building societies resulted in a low level for the index, but this increased with the conversion of Abbey National to a com-

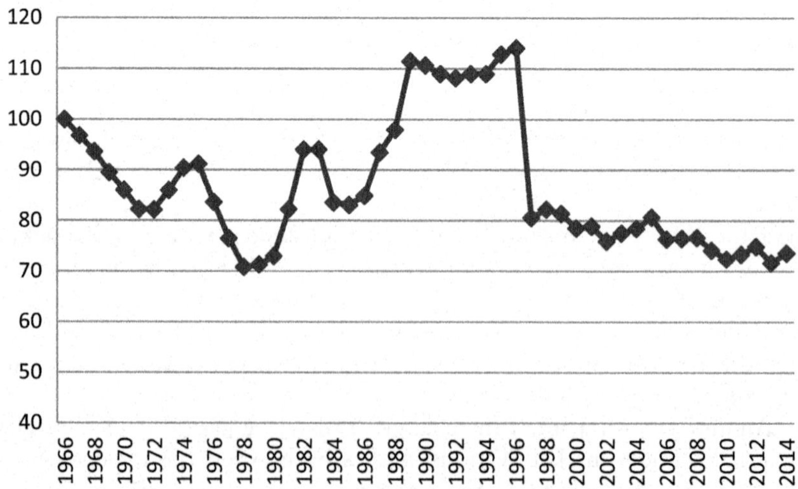

Fig. 2.2 Corporate diversity index for the UK mortgage market (*Source*: Data from BSA and Bank of England. Authors' calculations)

pany in 1989. This conversion served to improve the balance of ownership in the mortgage market, making it the most diverse it has been over the 50-year period. Unfortunately, this moment of relative diversity coincided with the early 1990s housing market crash. The demutualisations of the late 1990s, which included the Halifax—the largest lender in the country—tipped the balance the other way, and the market became dominated by plc banks. Subsequent changes in market share and ownership have led to further gradual declines in ownership diversity in the mortgage market.

In addition to the demutualisations, the trend for consolidation within the building society sector continued, as it had done for many decades, when boards of directors of some societies made the strategic decision that the interests of their members would be better served as part of a larger society. Members of the smaller society typically received a modest bonus to compensate them for the loss of their society's brand into the larger society.

2.4 Building Societies Through the Financial Crisis and Recession

The building society sector was not immune to the effects of the crisis, although to a different extent compared to banks. As early as 2006, the APPG for Building Societies and Financial Mutuals had noted that competitive pressures were putting increasing strain on the mutual model (APPG 2006). This pressure might have resulted in some boards looking at ways to keep pace with competitors, therefore increasing risk-taking, but without the necessary governance or controls, causing a number of building societies to run into trouble when the financial crisis unfolded.

The consolidation of the building society sector continued after the financial crisis hit. However, the nature of mergers changed as societies that ran into problems were typically merged with a larger, stronger society, but in order to preserve capital no bonus payments were made to members of the acquired society. The main causes for the mergers were various: losses on loans (particularly commercial loan books); losses due to potential fraud by borrowers becoming apparent; large deposits held with Icelandic banks; the low-interest-rate environment causing losses (particularly due to products contractually linked to base rate); losses on mortgage books acquired from other lenders prior to the crash and, in one case, the mis-selling of financial products from other providers. The generally low level of profit due to the prevailing economic environment meant that any of these problems were difficult to deal with. Table 2.3 lists the transfers of engagements since 2008.

Table 2.3 Transfers of engagements: 2008–2015

Year	*Transferee*	*Merged into*	*Date of transfer*	*Size ranking of transferee (2007 asset order)*	*Notes*
2014	City of Derry Building Society	Progressive Building Society	01/07/2014	58	
2013	Shepshed Building Society	Nottingham Building Society	01/07/2013	54	
	Century Building Society	Scottish Building Society	01/02/2013	59	
2011	Norwich & Peterborough Building Society	Yorkshire Building Society	01/11/2011	13	
	Kent Reliance Building Society	OneSavings Bank plc, part of the Kent Reliance Provident Society Group	01/02/2011	18	Society transferred assets and liabilities to new bank; membership to a new mutual Industrial & Provident Society, via the Butterfill Act. The bank was joint owned by the mutual and the external capital providers, which subsequently became the majority shareholder OneSavings Bank listed on the London Stock Exchange in June 2014

(*continued*)

Table 2.3 (continued)

Year	*Transferee*	*Merged into*	*Date of transfer*	*Size ranking of transferee (2007 asset order)*	*Notes*
2010	Stroud & Swindon Building Society	Coventry Building Society	01/09/2010	15	
	Chesham Building Society	Skipton Building Society	01/06/2010	42	
	Chelsea Building Society	Yorkshire Building Society	01/04/2010	5	
2009	Britannia Building Society	The Co-operative Financial Services	01/08/2009	2	Via the Butterfill Act
	Dunfermline Building Society	Nationwide Building Society	31/03/2009	14	Dunfermline's savings accounts, branches, head office, and the majority of its residential mortgage book were transferred to Nationwide on 30 March 2009, and the social housing portfolio was acquired from DBS Bridge Bank, established under the Bank of England, on 1 July 2009. The remainder of the business, including acquired mortgages and the commercial loan business were placed into a Building Society Special Administration Process
	Scarborough Building Society	Skipton Building Society	31/03/2009	17	

(*continued*)

Table 2.3 (continued)

Year	*Transferee*	*Merged into*	*Date of transfer*	*Size ranking of transferee (2007 asset order)*	*Notes*
2008	Barnsley Building Society	Yorkshire Building Society	31/12/2008	34	
	Catholic Building Society	Chelsea Building Society	31/12/2008	57	
	Cheshire Building Society	Nationwide Building Society	15/12/2008	11	
	Derbyshire Building Society	Nationwide Building Society	01/12/2008	9	

Note: The Building Societies (Funding) and Mutual Societies (Transfers) Act of 2007, also known as the Butterfill Act, allowed mergers between different types of mutual. Details on the provisions of the Butterfill Act are provided in Sect. 3.3

As shown in Table 2.4, size was not a good indicator of which societies would run into problems. Although some of the smallest societies did ultimately seek mergers, these tended to be in the latter stages of the crisis period. Those societies that ran into problems in the immediate aftermath of the financial crisis were often large- to medium-sized societies which may have attempted, in the early 2000s, to keep up with peers in the building society sector, or even the demutualised plc sector, by expanding into areas that they did not fully understand or had the capability to manage.

It is worth highlighting that not all societies that diversified away from traditional mortgage lending necessarily had to merge. Indeed, some diversifications, such as estate and lettings agency businesses, helped societies by providing an alternative source of earnings through the crisis and subsequent recession. Many others had diversified their lending activity in some way, including into commercial or self-certified loans, but any losses were manageable for the society as a whole.

Today the building society sector is very concentrated, particularly so after the financial crisis (see Table 2.3). After the demutualisation of Bradford & Bingley in 2000, the five largest societies accounted for 68 %

Table 2.4 Size and rank of Merged Building Societies (2008–2015)

Size rank (2007 assets)	*Number of societies merged (2008–2015)*	*Merged societies (proportion of number in 2007 band) (%)*
Top 10	3	30
11–20	6	60
21–30	0	0
31–40	1	10
41–50	1	10
51–59	4	44

of the sector's assets. By 2014, this had increased to 88%. Nationwide Building Society is by far the largest society, accounting for almost 60% of the sector's assets.

2.5 Sector Support

Whereas the failures of publicly quoted banks resulted in the government having to step in, in almost all instances of problems of building societies the sector supported itself by a larger society taking on the one with problems. The fact that this made commercial sense indicates that the underlying business was deemed viable, despite the issues at the time, and it also highlights the generally strong position of the larger societies.

The exception to the ability of the sector to support itself was the case of Dunfermline Building Society in 2009. Kent Reliance also received capital from outside the sector, but from private equity rather than the government.

Dunfermline had announced it would make an expected loss in 2008 due to its considerable commercial property loans and the mortgage books it had bought from GMAC and Lehmans, plus an Information Technology (IT) investment that had not gone to plan. Mergers with larger building societies were explored, as was a capital injection (to be drawn 50% from a consortium of large societies and 50% from the government), but neither came to fruition.

Instead, the Tripartite (HM Treasury, the Financial Services Authority (FSA), and the Bank of England (BOE)) used their new resolution powers under the recently enacted Banking Act 2009 to take the Dunfermline through the Special Resolution Regime. Dunfermline's savings accounts, branches, head office, and the majority of its residential mortgage book were transferred to Nationwide on 30 March 2009, with £1.6 billion of funding being supplied by the government to match the assets transferred. Dunfermline's social housing portfolio was acquired by Nationwide from DBS Bridge Bank, established under the BOE, on 1 July 2009. The remainder of the business, including acquired mortgages and the commercial loan business were placed into a Building Society Special Administration Process.

A review of the Dunfermline's failure was conducted by the Commons' Scottish Affairs Committee in 2009, which disclosed that the FSA considered a £30 million injection of external capital from the sector would have kept the society going in the short term, but that £60 million or more may have been required to give Dunfermline a longer-term future. However, the society's ability to service this capital injection was questioned by the regulator (Scottish Affairs Committee 2009). In hindsight, however, the cost of financing the notional loan to Financial Services Compensation Scheme (FSCS) in respect of Dunfermline is likely to far exceed these sums.[1]

It is important to point out that the government's direct support to DBS is small in comparison to the capital injections required by various banks. Following the run on Northern Rock, the government was required to step in and take the bank into public ownership in 2008. It was later restructured, with a £1.4 billion equity injection and over £20 billion in loans. Also in 2008, £37 billion of loans were supplied to Bradford & Bingley when it was nationalised. At three points over 2008–2009 the government took stakes in RBS and the newly formed Lloyds Banking Group, which amounted to £46 billion and £20 billion respectively (Jarrett 2010).

And while other forms of government system-wide support during the crisis were open to and used by some building societies, unsurprisingly the main beneficiaries were the big banks. The BOE's Special Liquidity Scheme (allowing banks and building societies to swap illiquid assets such as Mortgage Backed Securities for Treasury Bills) was open to building societies, as was the government's Credit Guarantee Scheme (guaranteeing short- and medium-term debt issuance by banks and building societies) but the Asset Protection Scheme was used by RBS and Lloyds banks only.

Of course, the eventual restoration of confidence in the system as a whole benefited all firms. But the expectation that the UK government would have to stand behind its biggest banks remained, and was manifest in the relative size of implicit subsidies for these firms in the financial system. The BOE estimated that in 2009, at the height of the crisis, large banks had an implicit subsidy of £102 billion, whereas the subsidy for the largest building societies together was just £2 billion (Bank of England 2010).

2.6 Conclusion

Building societies are specialist financial institutions with almost 250 years of history. They are mutual financial institutions owned by their customers. In its long history, the sector has faced many challenges, the most recent during the global financial crisis. Building societies, as well as banks, were severely impacted by the financial markets turbulence of 2007–2008. A number of building societies ran into trouble, particularly medium-sized institutions which may have attempted to keep up with larger peers in the building society sector and with the demutualised plc sector, by expanding into riskier areas. Unlike in the banking sector, direct government intervention was limited to the case of the DBS in 2009. By and large, the sector supported itself by larger societies taking on troubled ones. This led to further consolidation in the sector, with 15 mergers occurring since 2008.

Notes

1. Under the Special Resolution Regime, there was no direct loan to FSCS, unlike the calls on the FSCS in 2008 relating to B&B and the Icelandic banks. Instead, the FSCS was liable for any shortfall from the recovery of Dunfermline assets that did not cover the government's funding which had been applicable to insured deposits. A fixed 4.5 % rate of interest was charged on the notional loan.

References

APPG. (2006). Windfalls or shortfalls? The true cost of demutualisation. Short inquiry. All Party Parliamentary Group for Building Societies and Financial Mutuals. March.

Ayadi, R., Llewellyn, D., & Schmidt, R. (2010a). Investigating diversity in European banking: The role of cooperative banks. Centre for European Policy Studies.

Ayadi, R., Llewellyn, D., Schmidt, R.H., Arbak, E., & de Groen, W.P. (2010b). Investigating diversity in the banking sector in Europe: Key developments, performance and role of cooperative banks. Brussels: Centre for European Policy Studies Banking and Finance, No. 28.

Bank of England. (2010). Financial stability report. December 2010.

Boleat, M. (1981). The building society industry. Routledge, London.

Cable, V. (2012). Building Britain out of the slump: 80 years on, speech delivered to CentreForum. http://www.centreforum.org/index.php/mainrecent/365-building-britain-slump-80-years-on. Accessed 8 Oct 2015.

Cleary, E. J. (1965). *The building society movement*. London: Elek.

Coles, A. (2013). 30 years... and counting, BSA yearbook 2013/14. Building Societies Association.

Haldane, A., & May, R. (2011). Systemic risk in banking ecosystems. *Nature, 469*, 351–355.

House of Commons Papers. (2009). Fifth report, Dunfermline building society. House of Commons, Scottish Affairs Committee. Stationery Office Books (30 July 2009).

Jarrett, T. (2010). Taxpayer direct support to banks. House of Commons Library.

Michie, J., & Oughton, C. (2013). Investigating diversity in financial services markets: A divesity index. Centre for Financial and Management Studies Discussion Paper Series.

Shiwakoti, R. (2005). Building societies' demutualisation and managerial private interest. Kent Business School Working Paper.

CHAPTER 3

Legislation, Regulation, and Governance of Building Societies

Abstract Building societies are mutual financial institutions, owned by their members. They are also known as stakeholder-based financial institutions, and together with co-operatives and saving banks, form an important share of the financial sector in many countries. This chapter reviews the legal and regulatory framework with respect to building societies' permissible activities and discusses recent developments. In addition, we consider the strengths and weaknesses of the building society model, with a particular focus on capital and governance.

3.1 Introduction

Co-operatives, savings, and mutual financial institutions have a long history in most developed countries. These institutions, also known as stakeholder-based financial institutions, represent an important share of the banking sector in many countries. Although technically speaking, building societies in the UK are not co-operative banks (not the least because, by regulation, they are not "banks" and do not offer the full range of banking services), as mutuals they are a subset of stakeholder-based financial institutions (Ayadi et al. 2010a).

Building societies are mutual organisations, owned by their members. The UK building societies sector is legislated by the Building Societies Act 1986 and subsequent amendments.[1] The 1986 Act (Section 5(1)) provides that a building society may be established under the 1986 Act if (and only if)—

B. Casu, A. Gall, *Building Societies in the Financial Services Industry*,
DOI 10.1057/978-1-137-60208-4_3

> Its purpose or principal purpose is that of making loans which are secured on residential property and are funded substantially by its members

Building societies used to be wholly focused on personal savings and housing finance. Following the deregulation in the 1980s, they became more integrated into the overall financial system, although this also meant they faced increased competition from commercial banks, as the latter were increasing their share of the mortgage market. Even today, they remain highly specialised mutual institutions.

Although subsequent legislation has relaxed some of the constraints on building societies' permissible activities, they are still faced with some notable restrictions, including:

- the lending limit: at least 75% of the "business assets" of a building society must be loans fully secured on residential property (Section 6 of the Act).
- the funding limit: at least 50% of the funds of a building society must be raised in the form of shares held by individual members of the society (Section 7 of the Act)
- the limit of the powers a building society in relation to acting as a market maker in securities, commodities, or currencies; trading in commodities or currencies; and entering into transactions involving derivatives (Section 9A of the Act).

Unlike commercial banks, ownership is not based on shareholders but on membership. As progressive liberalisation of the restrictions imposed on the activities a mutual can undertake has taken place, it is often argued that the key difference between stakeholder-based financial institutions and shareholder-oriented commercial banks lies in the objectives pursued by managers. While the key objective for commercial banks is shareholders' wealth maximisation, managers of stakeholder-based financial institutions have to fulfil different targets, ranging from providing banking services to specific geographical areas, professions or individuals with specific characteristics. However, this does not imply that managers of stakeholder-based financial institutions do not have in their remit profit generation, insofar that profit is related to the institution's solvency and growth prospects. This is also known as a "double bottom line," that is, where profit maximisation has to be combined with social and other objectives (Anguren Martin and Marques Sevillano, 2011).

In the remainder of this chapter, we will discuss the legal and regulatory framework of building societies in more detail, with the aim to understand the sector's unique challenges. We will also present a discussion of the key issues concerning the governance of building societies.

3.2 The Legal and Regulatory Framework

The Building Societies Act 1986, as originally enacted, was prescriptive in respect of building societies' powers and the way in which they were exercised. However, the Act also gave numerous powers to a newly formed building societies' supervisory authority, the Building Societies Commission, as well as HM Treasury, to amend the provisions of the 1986 Act via Statutory Instruments, subject to Parliamentary approval. The 1986 Act also enabled societies to convert to publicly quoted companies.

The 1986 Act has been amended over time, most notably in 1997, which changed the prescriptive nature of the 1986 Act to a permissive regime whereby a building society could engage in a wide range of commercial activities subject to a building society's principal purpose, as well as so-called balance sheet "nature limits" and restrictions on powers. These changes increased the commercial freedom of societies, with the aim of enhancing competition and consumer choice. Some of the most important parts of the legislation are described below.

(i) Principal purpose

Section 5 of the Act provides that a building society may be established if (and only if) "its purpose or principal purpose is that of making loans which are secured on residential property and are funded substantially by its members."

(ii) Balance sheet limits

(a) *The lending limit*

Section 6 provides that at least 75% of the "business assets" of a building society must be loans fully secured on residential property. "Business assets" are total assets plus provisions for bad and doubtful debts, less fixed assets, liquid assets, and any long-term insurance funds.

(b) ***The funding limit***
Section 7 provides that at least 50% of the funds of a building society must be raised in the form of shares held by individual members of the society. This therefore limits a society's ability to raise funds from wholesale markets.

These limits have a clear impact on the structure of building societies' balance sheets. As Fig. 3.1 shows, building societies' balance sheets have always been predominantly mortgage loans secured on residential property, as is required by the lending limit. Through the 1990s, societies began to diversify into other forms of lending, and this limited diversification remains in 2014, though the composition of the assets will have changed. Many societies have reduced commercial loan books after the financial crisis, for example.

Liquid assets had remained at a broadly stable proportion over the period, but has declined in recent years as Treasury Bills drawn from the Funding for Lending Scheme (FLS) are held off-balance sheet (OBS), but reduce a society's requirement to hold sovereign bonds for liquidity purposes, and also because the Financial Services Authority relaxed its approach to liquidity and encouraged banks and building societies not to hold excess liquid assets, particularly as the Bank of England's new liquidity facilities could be relied upon in times of stress if firms had prepositioned collateral at the Bank (Financial Services Authority 2012).

On the funding side, the reliance on deposits from members is also clear. The liberalisation that began in 1983 enabled building societies to raise funding on the wholesale markets and, up to a limit, societies took the opportunity to diversify their funding to varying extents by issuing bonds and notes, certificates of deposit, securitisations, and covered bonds. The use of wholesale funding across the sector grew in the run-up to the financial crisis, as shown in Fig. 3.1. The limit in legislation is that non-member funding could make up to 50% of all funding; in practice, the highest the sector average arrived at was just above 30%. The credit crunch and subsequent changes to the market and regulation have meant that the latest figure shows less than 20% of building society funding is from wholesale sources, on average.

(iii) **Restrictions on powers**

Section 9A of the Act imposes restrictions, subject to certain exceptions, on the powers of a building society in relation to acting as a market

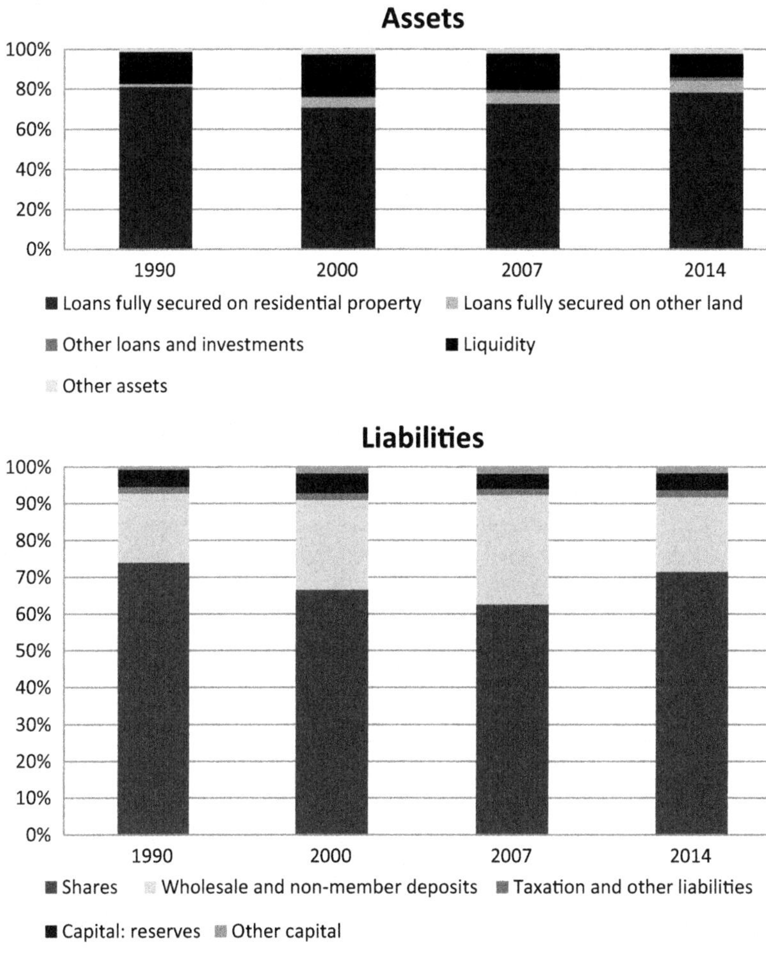

Fig. 3.1 Building society balance sheet structure (*Source*: BSA and FSA. Note: Other capital includes Permanent Interest Bearing Shares (PIBS), Profit Participating Deferred Shares (PPDS) and Core Capital Deferred Shares (CCDS))

maker in securities, commodities, or currencies; trading in commodities or currencies; and entering into transactions involving derivatives. The main exceptions relate to hedging a society's own risks, or a customer's risks, typically through interest rate, currency, or credit default swaps. However, societies cannot write derivatives to assume risk.

(iv) **Member democracy**

Schedule 2 to the 1986 Act makes rules covering a society's internal regulation and arrangements concerning membership, meetings, resolutions, and the appointment of directors. Most people who have a savings account or a mortgage with a building society automatically become a member. Members have rights to receive notice of, take part in and vote at the society's Annual General Meeting (AGM), where they can vote to approve the annual report and accounts, appoint the auditors, and elect directors to the board. All societies also now voluntarily hold a vote on the Directors' Remuneration policy. Members have one vote, regardless of the amount they have saved with or borrowed from the society—the principle of one member, one vote.

Members can also put forward resolutions to be discussed at the AGM, or they can request a Special General Meeting be held, subject to meeting certain conditions such as getting the support of a number of other members. Members can also nominate a candidate for election as a director of the society. Members are also entitled to receive a range of information, such as a copy of the annual Summary Financial Statement on the society's business or the full Annual Report.

3.2.1 Regulatory Bodies

The 1986 Act established the Building Societies Commission as the regulator for building societies, replacing the Chief Registrar of Friendly Societies, which had been in existence in some form since 1836.

In 2000–2001, the FSA was established as a new regulator for banks, building societies, and various other financial service providers, replacing the sector's own specific regulator. As such, the building society sector was subject to the same regulations as its banking competitors on capital, liquidity, and conduct and authorisations, as it has been since.

The FSA was broken up in 2013 in the wake of the financial crisis of 2007–2008 into the Prudential Regulatory Authority (PRA), a subsidiary of the BOE responsible for ensuring the soundness of individual firms, and the independent Financial Conduct Authority (FCA), whose remit is to regulate firms' behaviour. Among the new regulators' objectives are goals to promote or facilitate effective competition, which is a new area of accountability for both. A new Financial Policy Committee (FPC) was also established in the BOE as a macro-prudential regulator to monitor and mitigate risks across the financial system as a whole.

There are some differences in building societies' regulatory position. In 2010, the FSA introduced a *Specialist Sourcebook for Building Societies.* This guidance was in response to some of the problems that had arisen in societies during the crisis, and put limits on a society's treasury operations and lending activities, unless the society can demonstrate the appropriate level of controls and risk management expertise covering credit, interest rate, basis, and treasury risks to satisfy the regulator. The Sourcebook sets out guidance for three approaches to lending (traditional, limited, and mitigated), and outlines five treasury management approaches (administered, matched, extended, comprehensive, and trading). While it is difficult to object to the principle of the Sourcebook, it is not obvious why it applies to building societies exclusively and not to other firms. In fact, it provides guidance on the same prudential regime that applies to banks. In 2016 the Sourcebook will be reviewed, but is set to remain in place for societies.

The increased regulatory burden predates the financial crisis, with UK financial institutions subject to EU regulation stemming from the global Basel Committee on Banking Supervision (BCBS), for example. However, regulatory changes introduced in response to the crisis amplified this trend. Often European regulations, such as those relating to capital requirements, are on a "maximum harmonisation" basis meaning national regulators have no discretion in how the regulation is applied. There are questions, however, as to whether these regulations should apply equally to banks and mutuals. Building societies, in conjunction with co-operative and mutual banks in other countries, are seeking to influence regulatory design to ensure that mutual models are recognised adequately by regulators.

3.2.2 Other Recent Regulatory Reforms

The Building Societies (Funding) and Mutual Societies (Transfers) Act of 2007 was introduced as a Private Member's Bill by Sir John Butterfill MP and is therefore sometimes referred to as the Butterfill Act. It enabled the government (via secondary legislation) to amend building society legislation so that up to 75 % of funds could be borrowed from wholesale markets and to change the creditor hierarchy so that members' shares would rank equally (pari passu) with liabilities to creditors in the event of insolvency (they had previously been subordinate). It also allowed mergers between different types of mutual, and this section was brought into force in 2009 in time for Britannia's merger with the Co-operative Bank. The secondary legislation that required to implement the higher 75 % limit on non-member funding has never been introduced.

As part of the UK implementation of the EU's Bank Recovery and Resolution Directive, insured depositors, including members' shares, were given preference in the creditor hierarchy by an Order that came into force in 2015, therefore leapfrogging the intentions of the Butterfill Act.

As discussed in Chap. 1, in 2010 the coalition government (2010–2015) established the Independent Commission on Banking (ICB), chaired by the economist John Vickers, to investigate how the structure of banking could be made safer following the financial crisis. The ICB recommended that the retail banking activities were ring-fenced so that they could easily be separated from more risky investment banking activities. It was considered whether building societies should be covered by ring-fencing, but the government decided that the restrictions in the Building Societies Act effectively limited their activity already and imposing an additional legal separation on the sector would be largely irrelevant, so societies were carved out of the ring-fencing requirements.

Finally, a 2012 Parliamentary Commission on Banking Standards made recommendations that resulted in a new Senior Managers Regime and a Certification regime which are being implemented by the PRA and FCA by 2016, which is imposing a considerable burden on all affected firms.

3.3 Building Societies' Capital

Building societies, as mutuals owned by their customers, cannot readily raise external capital and instead must rely on accumulating reserves of retained profit, historically referred to as surplus. As a result, most of building societies' high-quality Common Equity Tier 1 (CET1) capital is retained profit built up over generations. As opposed to issued share capital, no returns need to be generated in order to pay dividends. This has a number of implications. The challenges building societies face in raising external capital tend to make them more risk averse, as demonstrated by their generally lower levels of mortgage arrears and higher levels of capital compared to their banking counterparts, with building society boards keen to maintain conservative capital positions. The sector average gross capital ratio, expressed as a percentage of all shares, deposits, and loans, reached 6.88 % in 2014, the highest level since 1997. The absence of pressure to make returns to shareholders may also mean societies avoid the short-termism that banks are sometimes accused of.

However, building societies have issued limited amounts of certain capital instruments. Raising a limited amount of inorganic capital gives societies greater flexibility to respond to opportunities and events. It is important that capital instruments preserve the principle of mutuality and do not alter the purpose of the organisation towards maximising returns to providers of external capital. Investors in the instruments are members of the building society, and are subject to the principle of one member, one vote, regardless of the size of their holding.

Below we discuss some of these instruments: Permanent Interest Bearing Shares (PIBS); Profit Participating Deferred Shares (PPDS); and Core Capital Deferred Shares (CCDS).

Permanent Interest Bearing Shares (PIBS)

PIBS were issued by a number of (mainly larger) societies in the 1990s, but these were deemed not to be sufficiently capable of absorbing losses to qualify as CET1 capital under regulatory requirements that became more stringent in the wake of the financial crisis. The EU's Capital Requirements Regulation (CRR) required that, to qualify as CET1, capital instruments must be perpetual, loss absorbing, subordinate to all other claims, and have completely variable returns. This final requirement is the most troublesome for mutuals as building society members rather than providers of external capital should benefit from residual profits. As a result of lobbying by the European Association of Co-operative Banks, this and certain other provisions were modified for mutuals and co-operative banks.

Profit Participating Deferred Shares (PPDS)

A few societies currently have PPDS as a result of capital restructurings during the crisis and these do qualify, but none of these have been issued independently. PPDS have a discretionary, capped dividend, and are loss absorbing so qualify as CET1 capital, but may be difficult to market to new investors.

Core Capital Deferred Shares (CCDS)

Nationwide Building Society developed and issued a new instrument, CCDS, which satisfies the regulators' latest requirements to qualify as

CET1. It is also consistent with the mutual model, as the coupon is capped and discretionary. Nationwide's 2013 issue of £550 million of CCDS to professional investors was oversubscribed, and had an initial distribution cap set at 15%. Each holder of CCDS has one vote, regardless of the number of CCDS held, though in practice Nationwide's CCDS holders are only entitled to one vote in total for all issued CCDS as the CCDS are held via a custodian who agreed to waive this voting right.

Other societies have issued lower ranking Additional Tier 1 (AT1) instruments that could convert to CCDS, but no other society has currently issued CCDS. In 2015, the conduct regulator, the FCA, approved the limited sale of CCDS to retail investors subject to certain safeguards, which could open up the possibility of other, smaller societies issuing CCDS, though no such sale has yet taken place.

3.3.1 Leverage Ratio

Building societies are required by law to focus on residential mortgage lending, so their balance sheets are generally less risky than banks that have considerable commercial or unsecured lending, for example. They are therefore generally well capitalised relative to banks on a risk-weighted basis, as prime residential mortgages attract a low-risk weight. However, as a leverage ratio of equity to assets deliberately ignores the riskiness of assets, it could be argued that institutions with a high proportion of lower-risk assets are effectively discriminated against.

In 2013, the PRA introduced a 3% minimum non-risk-weighted leverage ratio, to supplement the risk-weighted capital regime. This was applied to the eight major financial institutions, which included Nationwide Building Society. At the time, Nationwide was required to explain how it planned to improve its leverage ratio, which it then achieved ahead of schedule.

The Chancellor then asked the FPC to conduct a review of the leverage ratio, with a view to introducing requirements in the UK ahead of the relevant European legislation. The FPC completed its review in 2014, and was granted powers to set the leverage ratio in 2015. The FPC proposed a 3% minimum with additional buffers, but using a tighter definition for eligible capital (with just 25% of AT1 capital allowable for the minimum requirement, none for the buffers) than was the case in the draft European legislation (which allowed all Tier 1). Initially the minimum leverage ratio will cover just banks and building societies with deposits of £50 billion or more, so catching just one building society, but the FPC intends that it should cover all firms in coming years once international requirements are defined.

3.4 The Contribution of Building Societies to Financial Stability

As discussed in Sect. 3.3, building societies cannot readily raise external capital. As a result, most of building societies' capital is retained earnings built up over time and which does not need to be remunerated. This creates both challenges and opportunities. The challenge is raising external funds: this difficulty makes building societies generally more risk averse and more likely to maintain conservative capital positions. Some argue that the absence of pressure to make returns to shareholders may mean societies avoid the short-termism that shareholder-oriented institutions are sometimes accused of. Some authors (see Ayadi et al. 2009) have also argued that this characteristic might make mutuals better at mitigating risk on an inter-temporal basis, as they tend to accumulate less risk through the cycle. This is often seen as a positive contribution to the stability of the overall financial sector (Michie and Llewellyn 2010).

Academic research indicates that during the global financial crisis, co-operative banks faired comparatively well (Hesse and Cihak 2007; Ayadi et al. 2010a, b; Groeneveld and de Vries 2009). This was attributed to their business model and governance mechanisms, which follow a longer-term perspective, as they do not have to deliver short-term returns to shareholders. A recent study by Chiaramonte et al. (2015) finds that co-operative banks and other mutual financial institutions contribute positively to financial stability, but only above a certain market threshold.

The contribution of co-operative and mutual institutions to financial stability, however, remains controversial. As managers are less exposed to market discipline, this could lead to high level of inefficiency in the sector. This, in turn, can have a negative impact on innovation, on the adoption of new technology and on diversification of both funding and income sources.

In addition, some studies suggest that mutuals may find it more difficult to implement changes in response to adverse circumstances. For example, the Swedish co-operative banking sector did not survive the crisis of the early 1990s, since it faced high marginal costs of capital. Brunner et al. (2004) note that the need to restore capital was a major factor in the decision to demutualise in the Swedish case. Mutuals may be more vulnerable to shocks in credit quality and interest rates, since they are less diversified than commercial banks (Fonteyne 2007).

In the debate on the advantages and disadvantages of stakeholder-based financial institutions, a main argument relates to the need to foster and maintain diversity in the sector. A report prepared by Ayadi et al. (2010b) argues that preserving a multiplicity of aims within banking—a sort of biodiversity of banks—should be a paramount objective for policymakers. The main arguments for maintaining diversity in the financial sector include:

- improving access to financial services
- fostering regional development
- mitigating inter-temporal risks
- capitalising on the value of diversity
- stability of earnings

As one of the key criticisms to the building society model is the fact that mutuals are less exposed to market discipline, possibly leading to inefficiencies, in the next section we review the key issues related to the governance of building societies.

3.5 Governance of Building Societies

External discipline on building societies has sharpened over several decades. The end of the recommended rates arrangements clearly led to the advent of product market competition to meet the needs of consumers. More recently, the widespread application and knowledge of deposit insurance reduces the incentives for depositors to worry about the riskiness of the institution with which they save their money, which may previously have benefited building societies. More efficient communications mean that firms' conduct, pricing, accessibility, and so on, are under greater scrutiny than ever before.

And internal governance arrangements have also developed over time. In the original building societies, governance arose from the discipline that came from all members living in the same community. If someone were to abuse their position, they would face the social opprobrium of their fellow members. However, as societies grew in size and scope, governance arrangements became more sophisticated and more formal. The rights of members are now enshrined in legislation, as described above. And societies are required by the regulator to have regard to the UK Corporate Governance Code, even though this is designed for listed companies. One of the roles of Building Societies Association (BSA) roles is to help societies to interpret the Code for a mutual organisation.

However, history, not least in the years since 2008, has repeatedly shown that being mutually owned by customers is no guarantee for a firm's success or good governance. Yet, the centrality of customers, as owners, can help to reduce problems of misaligned incentives.

At a publicly quoted bank, the interests of shareholders and customers may conflict, but at a building society the owner and the customer are one and the same so this conflict does not arise. Of course there will be differences in opinions across the membership or customer base—between borrowers and savers, for example—and these need to be balanced, but at a building society they do not need also to be set against the interests of shareholders. The distinction is reflected in the Halifax Building Society board's proposal to convert in 1997:

> The owner of a business is concerned with matters such as whether the business is being effectively and efficiently managed, whether policies are in place to develop the business and whether the return received on his or her investment is adequate. In contrast, the concerns associated with being a customer of a business are different. The customer is concerned mainly with quality of service, convenience of distribution outlets, price and whether or not products meet his or her needs. Customers and owners have different priorities and the Board believes that this should be reflected in the constitution adopted by Halifax.
>
> (Halifax Building Society, 1997)

A particular risk is that dominant groups within the ownership, such as large shareholders in a plc, can push for strategies to be pursued that boost short-term performance but that may be at other stakeholders' expense, or may not be in the company's best long-term interests. Shareholders enjoy limited liability, which limits their potential losses and incentivises this.

Another potential governance problem arises from the separation of ownership—whether by shareholders or members—and the managers who control the day-to-day operations. Managers of banks have increasingly had their remuneration linked to the share price of the company to align their interests with shareholders. This is not as easily achieved at building societies that lack external capital, removing an incentive for risk-taking that is present at banks. Even if some form of mutual capital instrument were used, the returns are capped, thus limiting this incentive.

A criticism of member democracy and the one member, one vote principle is that a widely dispersed membership can exert little effective control over management. It could be argued that the major problems at banks demonstrated that shareholder ownership does not ensure effective control either. This prompted the government to commission the Kay Review into UK Equity markets and long-term decision making in 2011 (Kay 2012). The Review concluded that a decline in trust relationships and misaligned incentives had made short-termism a problem in equity investment, with lower quality engagement of shareholders and increased intermediation due to more dispersed and disinterested asset managers having replaced large pension or insurance funds as owners. The challenge of getting owners to participate in governance is therefore not exclusive to mutuals.

Building societies have invested a lot of resources in encouraging their members to engage in the governance of their society, though not every single member needs to be actively engaged as long as an appropriate and effective board is appointed to represent their interests.

The demutualisations were a wake-up call to societies that the value of member ownership needed to be demonstrated to members. In the decades since societies have invested in new ways to encourage members to participate and interact with the society and its board of directors. Increasingly, active and engaged members that have a relationship with the society are also seen as an important resource for strategic and operational decisions. A number of societies have member panels and forums that are used to test ideas and can impose tangible accountability as managers have to explain decisions to members (Building Societies Association 2015).

It seems that the nature of mutual ownership has evolved. Whereas the first building societies emerged as the organisational solution to meet a common need, today building societies must leverage their mutual values to deliver the products and approach that attract consumers and earn their loyalty before these customers participate as owners.

The governance arrangements at banks and building societies have a marked impact on organisational culture. The aforementioned quote from the Halifax conversion proposal indicates the shift in direction associated with the change in ownership. As the big banks look to restructure, they are implementing strategies that put the retail customer at the centre of their operations, apparently going full circle, and approaching familiar territory for building societies. It remains to be seen whether this is just marketing, or whether there will be real cultural change that is supported by changes to organisational structure and governance arrangements.

3.6 Conclusion

Building societies are mutual financial institutions with almost 250 years of history. The Building Societies Act 1986 describes the key purpose of building societies and establishes a number of legal limits to their operations. These include balance sheet nature limits, the lending limit and the funding limit, which shape the balance sheet structure of building societies. Following the post-crisis reforms, some building societies have had to increase their capital to comply with regulatory minimum. Although the sector is adequately capitalised, raising capital can be a challenge, as building societies must rely on accumulating reserves of retained profit. However, this constraint tends to make building societies generally more risk averse and therefore encourage them to maintain conservative capital positions. In addition, the lack of pressure to generate shareholders' returns can incentivise a long-term view, therefore encouraging mutuals to mitigate risks through the economic cycle. This is often seen as a positive contribution to the stability of the overall financial sector.

Notes

1. That Act has subsequently been revised by the Building Societies Act 1997, by the Financial Services and Markets Act 2000 and by the Financial Services Act 2012.

References

Anguren Martín, R. & Marqués Sevillano, J. M. (2011). Cooperative and savings banks in Europe: Nature, challenges and perspectives. Available at SSRN: http://ssrn.com/abstract=1856966

Ayadi, R., Arbak, E., Carbó Valverde, S., Rodriguez Fernandez, F., & Schmidt, R. H. (2009). *Investigating diversity in the banking sector in Europe: The performance and role of savings banks.* Brussels: Centre for European Policy Studies.

Brunner, A., Decressin, J., Hardy, D., & Kudela, B. (2004). Germany's three-pillar banking system—Cross-country perspective in Europe. International monetary fund occasional paper, no. 233.
Building Societies Association. (2015). Engaging conversations. Building Societies Association.
Chiaramonte, L., Poli, F., & Oriani, M. E. (2015). Are cooperative banks a lever for promoting bank stability? Evidence from the recent financial crisis in OECD countries. *European Financial Management, 21*(3), 491–523.
Financial Services Authority. (2012). Adjustments to FSA's liquidity and capital regime for UK banks and building societies, Statement on 27 Sept 2012. Financial Services Authority.
Fonteyne, W. (2007). Cooperative banks in Europe – Policy issues. International Monetary Fund working paper, WP/07/159.
Groeneveld, H., & de Vries, B. (2009). European co-operative banks: First lessons of the subprime crisis. *International Journal of Co-operative Management, 4*, 8–21.
Halifax Building Society. (1997). Transfer document. Halifax Building Society.
Hesse, H., & Cihak, M. (2007). Cooperative banks and financial stability. International Monetary Fund Working Paper.
Kay, J. (2012). The Kay review of UK equity markets and long term decision making: Final report. Department for Business, Innovation and Skills.
Michie, J., & Llewellyn, D. T. (2010). Converting failed institutions into mutual organisations. *Journal of Social Enterprise, 1*(1), 146–170.

CHAPTER 4

Financial Structure of the Building Society Sector

Abstract This chapter presents an analysis of the key issues faced by building societies in today's financial markets. We discuss the key changes in the structure of the industry and how these have impacted on margins and profitability and have resulted in restructuring and consolidation in the sector. Although banks and building societies broadly compete in the same markets and are subject to the same regulatory requirements, there are key differences in their business model. A building society's customers are also its owners. Recent studies highlight a higher degree of customers' satisfaction and trust in building societies compared to banks. This is also reflected in the lower amount of fines levied against societies for misconduct. While the overall outlook is positive, challenges remain, particularly arising from regulatory changes and financial innovation.

4.1 Introduction

The structure of the building society sector has changed substantially over recent decades. These changes went hand in hand with changes in building societies' financial performance over the period, notably changes due to increased competition in the mortgage market. Recall that up until the 1980s banks' ability to compete in the mortgage market had been constrained by an informal agreement not to compete, as well as regulatory constraints (see Sect. 2.3). The lack of competition and a system of agreed interest rates contributed to boosting societies' profitability. As these constraints were progressively relaxed during the 1980s, banks entered the

B. Casu, A. Gall, *Building Societies in the Financial Services Industry*,
DOI 10.1057/978-1-137-60208-4_4

mortgage market and began to compete for retail savings. The 1980s also saw the onset of price competition in the sector, with building societies no longer abiding by a system of suggested rates.

These changes are reflected in societies' net interest margins (NIMs), profitability, and efficiency. This chapter provides an analysis of these changes and sets the scene for the empirical analysis presented in Chap. 5.

4.2 Changes in Margins and Efficiency

In the 1970s and into the 1980s, the Council of the Building Societies Association (BSA) set interest rates so that margins covered the costs of doing business comfortably, including the costs of pursuing non-price service-based competition such as excessive branch growth. When the cartel broke down in the early to mid-1980s, the onset of competition took some time to feed through to profitability and efficiency.[1] Despite the more intense competition, margins increased slightly through the 1980s as societies, and their banking competitors, widened interest rate spreads against the backdrop of a booming housing market (Bank of England 1990). Meanwhile, diversification into new areas and new services, such as money transmission on some accounts, kept costs relatively high.

Interest rates rose in the late 1980s and into the 1990s to support the value of sterling to maintain the UK's membership of the Exchange Rate Mechanism. Between 1988 and 1990, the average building society mortgage rate had risen to 15.25% from 9.78%, causing many borrowers difficulties in repaying their mortgage. This was reflected in a rise in loan loss provisions at building societies when the economy entered recession, which fed through to a reduction in profitability.

Following the early 1990s recession, societies started on a long trend of improving the efficiency of their operations. There was an almost continual decline in the sector's management expenses ratio for two decades—from 140 pence per £100 of assets, to 76 pence by 2011—partly from cutting the excesses built up in the cartel years, partly from ongoing consolidation between societies, and partly from improving processes and introducing new technologies such as Automated Teller Machines (ATMs) and electronic communications.

In response to the demutualisations in the late 1990s, societies cut interest margins to demonstrate the benefits of mutuality through improved rates to members: building societies should enjoy an efficiency advantage relative to publicly quoted banks as they do not have to pay dividends to shareholders. In 1997, a year in which five large societies demutualised, the average NIM across the sector fell to 1.51 from 1.92 in the preceding year.

The continuing societies also narrowed margins, as competition intensified via new firms entering the mortgage market, a trend that was to continue through the following decade. Figure 4.1 illustrates these trends.

As the new millennium progressed, the intensity of competition in the mortgage market led to further gradual decline in margins and encouraged some societies, like banks, to expand in new directions: buying existing mortgage books, including of non-prime loans, commercial mortgages, and the growing buy-to-let sector.

Building societies also developed other income sources to supplement the interest income from their core business. These sources include mortgage-related fees and commission from the sale of insurance, often also linked to mortgage business. In the late 1980s and 1990s, endowment life insurance was a key product, but more recently, buildings and home contents insurance has become more prominent.

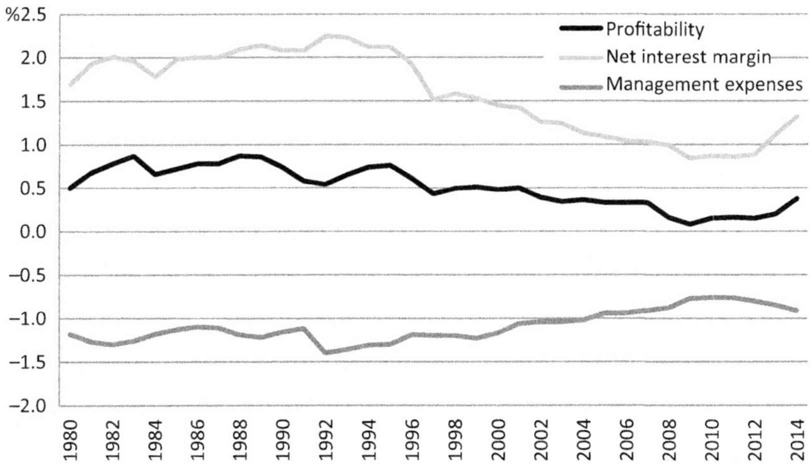

Fig. 4.1 Building societies' margins profitability and expenses (*Source*: BSA from 2009 and 1980–1999; Financial Services Authority 2000–2008). (Note: net interest margin (NIM), profitability, and management expenses as % of mean assets. Management expenses include administration, staffing costs, and depreciation. They are shown as negative.)

When the financial crisis intensified in October 2008 and seemed certain to affect the real economy, the response of the Monetary Policy Committee (MPC) at the Bank of England was to cut the Bank Rate dramatically from 5.0% to 0.5% by March 2009, six months later. This low rate was unprecedented in the Bank's 300-year history, and had a significant impact on the profitability of banks and building societies, which had mortgage and savings accounts with terms and conditions that were not written to deal with the base rate at this level. Savings rates were cut towards zero, but the spread between these and Bank Rate was squeezed. Many tracker mortgages became loss making; income derived from building societies' reserves of retained profit dropped significantly, and the returns on liquidity reduced as more liquidity was now being held on deposit at the BOE. When wholesale funding markets seized up, competition for stable retail funding increased, putting considerable pressure on deposit margins. Building societies' retained surplus (profit) in 2009 was just 8 pence for every £100 of assets. In the first eight years of the decade, it had averaged 36 pence; in the 1990s, it was 61 pence.

Another major drag on building society profitability in the years after the crisis was the contribution to the bailout of failed organisations via levies on banks and building societies to fund the interest payments on loans made by the government to the UK's deposit insurance scheme, the Financial Services Compensation Scheme (FSCS). The allocation of FSCS levies related to the size of each firm's retail deposit balances. As building societies rely on retail funding—as they are required to by legislation—they had to pay a disproportionately large share of the levies compared to banks that relied on wholesale funding, even though excessive reliance on this latter, less stable source of funds was one of the main causes of the financial crisis. In 2012, 61% of building societies charged more against their profits for the FSCS than they did for mortgage losses.

In response to the pressure on profitability, many societies cut their costs aggressively, as reflected in the reduction in the management expense ratio after the crisis. Once the worst of the crisis was over, however, societies began investing in systems and implementing the various regulatory reforms that had been introduced, which caused their management expense ratios to pick up again.

The introduction of the Funding for Lending Scheme (FLS) by the BOE and HM Treasury in 2012 led to a significant reduction in funding costs for banks and building societies. This helped to restore building society margins, even for societies that did not draw any money from the scheme, and profitability across the sector increased to 38 pence per £100 of assets in 2014.

4.3 Recent Changes in Mortgage Market Share

Figure 4.2 shows building societies' share of new mortgage lending, net of repayments—broadly equivalent to how much the stock of outstanding mortgage loans is growing each year—was around 16% in the period 2000–2005 (society only) and 19% in 2006–2008 (when data includes the lending subsidiaries of building societies). However, once the crisis and recession hit, at an aggregate level, societies withdrew from the mortgage market and as such their net lending was negative and their stock of outstanding mortgages reduced. As customer-owned organisations without

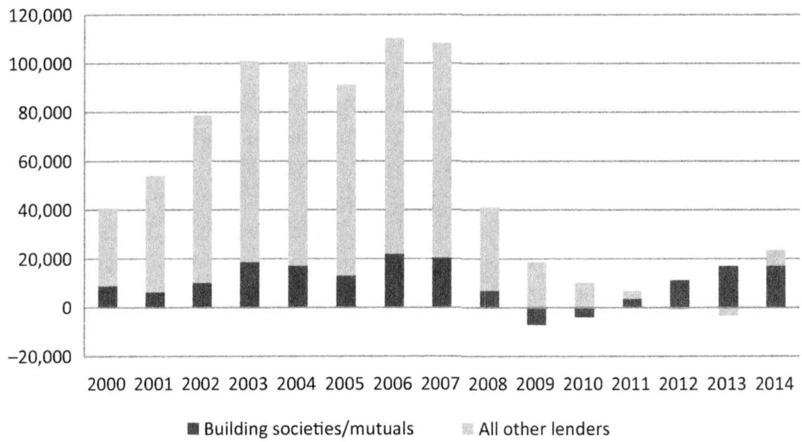

Fig. 4.2 UK net mortgage lending, £m (*Source*: Data from BSA and Bank of England; authors' calculations). (Note: prior to 2006 building society data does not include societies' lending subsidiaries. From 2006 onwards, societies' lending subsidiaries are included. Britannia is excluded from the building society sector from August 2009. Data from January 2010 to November 2013 inclusive is for the mutual sector, so includes lending by the Co-operative Bank. Data from December 2013 onwards is building society only, including their subsidiaries. Data for all other lenders in each period is calculated as the total market figure from the Bank of England less the building society/ mutual figure)

the pressure of making returns to shareholders, hunkering down until the worst of a crisis is over can be seen as an acceptable short-term strategy.

From the second half of 2011, the building society sector began to play a more important role in the mortgage market once again and in recent years have been responsible for the bulk of net lending across the UK. From 2011 to the end of 2014 around 90% of net lending was from building societies. In 2014, societies had net lending of £17 billion, similar to 2003–2004 levels but still somewhat short of their immediate pre-crisis level, which was over £20 billion. In contrast, net mortgage lending by all other lenders remained a fraction of net lending in more normal times.

In terms of share of outstanding mortgage balances, unsurprisingly the changes are much less dramatic, as net lending levels have remained in the tens of billions, compared to balances of £1.3 trillion. Having held an 80% share of outstanding mortgages at the end of the 1970s, the building society sector held just 20% following the demutualisation of Bradford & Bingley in 2000. Over the following years, this gradually reduced further due to the intensity of competition in the mortgage market. There are some breaks in the time series, which make direct comparisons difficult. However, if building society subsidiaries are included, just before the Britannia merger in 2009, the sector had a 20.1% share of balances, which dropped to 18.3% immediately after the merger. By the end of 2014, this had increased to 20.0%, and by the middle of 2015, the sector had a 20.3% share. The sector's strong lending in recent years has therefore made up for the effect of the Britannia leaving to join the Co-operative Bank.

4.4 Recent Changes in Savings Market Share

Whereas building societies' share of mortgage loans declined after 2000 before recovering in recent years, the sector's share of outstanding deposit balances has remained very stable since 2000, at around 20% of balances, with a share of the change in balances typically a little greater than this (see Fig. 4.3). Societies did not expand their use of wholesale funding to the same extent as other institutions, as mentioned in Chapter 2, leaving them less exposed during the credit crunch.

When doubts about the safety of certain banks began to emerge in 2007 and 2008, building societies, together with the government-owned National Savings & Investments (NS&I), benefited from being seen as relatively more secure and received a larger share of deposits from the

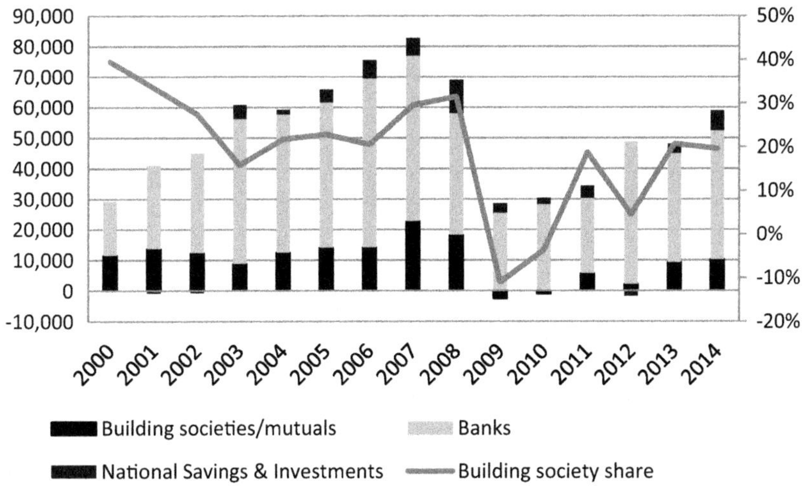

Fig. 4.3 Changes in UK household savings balances (*Source*: Data from BSA and Bank of England; authors' calculations). (Note that Britannia is excluded from the building society sector from August 2009. Data from January 2010 to November 2013 inclusive is for the mutual sector, so includes deposits with the Co-operative Bank. Data from December 2013 onwards is building society only. Data for banks and NS&I is from the Bank of England)

run on Northern Rock and the large volume of withdrawals from Halifax and Bradford & Bingley as their position was questioned by the media. However, once the government expanded deposit guarantees and it was believed that it would protect all deposits (though it never made this explicit), these inflows largely reversed. With the wholesale markets dysfunctional, competition for retail funding intensified. On average, societies saw small net outflows in 2009 and 2010.

It was not until the FLS was introduced in 2012 that funding conditions improved. The FLS enabled banks and building societies to pledge relatively illiquid assets as collateral with the Bank of England in exchange for liquid UK Treasury Bills that could be drawn for up to four years. A firm's capacity to borrow from the scheme and the price it paid were linked to lending volumes to try to stimulate activity in the mortgage market. The scheme was extended three times, but these extensions focused on lending to small businesses rather than mortgages. Twenty-eight building societies registered for the original FLS, though four did not draw any funds from it.

At the 2014 Budget, the Chancellor of the Exchequer announced that NS&I would offer market-beating rates on fixed rate savings bonds for pensioners. These were available for a limited period from January 2015, prompting claims that they were a political ploy. Initial Treasury estimates were that these Pensioner Bonds would attract £10 billion, but more than £13 billion was deposited. Building societies had raised concerns previously about NS&I's potential for distorting the savings market, given its government backing and certain tax advantages that some of its products enjoyed. The Pensioner Bonds were an extreme distortion, and though their issuance appears to have been a one-off, NS&I was set a considerable £10 billion net funding target for the 2015–2016 tax year.

4.5 Customer Satisfaction

The previous sections in this chapter have analysed various metrics based on the financial results of building societies. Banks and building societies compete in the same markets and are held to broadly the same regulatory requirements so the efficiency and performance of their businesses are important factors to consider.

However, other differences are often claimed relating to the way that building societies, co-operative, or other customer-owned banks approach their business objectives. A building society's customers are also its owners, so it might be expected that this would affect how its customers are treated and the approach the business takes to dealing with its customers. Common claims about the differences in building societies' conduct include that they tend to offer better levels of customer service; they receive fewer customer complaints and handle them better than other firms when they do receive them; and they are subject to significantly fewer fines for misconduct. Each of these in addressed in turn below.

Consumer surveys have consistently demonstrated a significant difference between building societies and banks on a number of service related factors. Some recent survey data is shown in Table 4.1. The data shows some sizeable differences in particular aspects, such as consumers' trust in their provider to act in their best interests, where building societies have a score 10 percentage points higher than banks. Similar margins are evident in terms of recommending to friends and family, treating customers fairly, being valued as a customer, and value for money.

Table 4.1 Customer satisfaction survey—Average (Q2:2014–Q4: 2015)

Service metric (% agreeing with the following statements)	*Building society (%)*	*Bank (%)*	*Difference (%)*
My provider provides good customer service	96	90	+6
The financial products offered by my provider are easy to understand	96	91	+5
I would recommend my provider to my friends and family	94	84	+9
I feel as though my provider treats me fairly as a customer	93	85	+8
My provider provides good value for money	93	84	+9
I can trust my provider to act in my best interests	91	81	+10
My provider offers competitive rates	91	81	+10
My provider treats me as an individual	87	79	+8
My provider makes me feel as though my business is valuable to them	86	76	+10

Source: Canadean Consumer, commissioned by the Building Societies Association. Each quarter, from June 2014 to December 2015, 2000 adults were interviewed online by Canadean Consumer. The figures were weighted and are representative of all UK adults (aged 18+). The figures in the table are the averages over the seven quarters, representing 14,000 adults. To avoid misallocation, respondents were asked to identify the brand they used for each of their main current account, savings account, and mortgage. They were then asked about the service at each of these brands. As a result the responses in the table above represent the opinions of consumers on 12,462 relationships with a bank and 3257 relationships with a building society

Researchers at Nottingham University Business School have studied trust in retail financial services providers over the last decade, and developed indices to measure trust and fairness (Devlin 2014). The indices are composed of survey measures of various dimensions of trust, fairness, and loyalty, and are split across various types of provider. The results consistently show a positive score for building societies on their trust and fairness indices, indicating that building societies are generally trusted by consumers, while banks have large negative scores (Devlin 2014).

Another indicator that might be indicative of the different position of customers at banks and building societies is to look at the instances when something has gone wrong, and how it is dealt with. The Financial Conduct Authority (FCA) collates statistics on complaints by firm, for those firms with over 500 complaints in a six-month period. Building societies tend to have a proportionately smaller share of complaints. For example, in the first half of 2015, they had 3% of all complaints while high street banks made up 67% of the total. The remainder were insurance companies, asset managers, and specialist lenders. However, banks clearly have a wider range of activities than building societies, including more widespread provision of current accounts, so might be expected to receive a larger number of complaints. Even if we drill down to look just at complaints relating to housing finance, building societies accounted for 16% of complaints in the first half of 2015—less than their 20% share of outstanding mortgage balances. Banks accounted for 65% and Other Lenders 19% (13% of which was UK Asset Resolution, the body administering the loan books of Northern Rock and Bradford & Bingley).

The Financial Ombudsman Service (FOS) is an independent organisation established to adjudicate on complaints that financial service providers do not resolve to their customers' satisfaction. A customer with a complaint must give his or her provider the opportunity to deal with the complaint in the first instance. However, if they are not satisfied with the outcome, they can take the complaint to FOS. FOS publishes statistics on the number of complaints it receives about each firm for every half-year period (above a threshold of 30 cases over six months). These data enable us to assess for which firms a complaint is more likely to go to the Ombudsman rather than being dealt with to the customer's satisfaction by the firm. The data also allow us to analyse whether FOS has resolved the complaint in favour of the firm or the customer.

Good customer service is likely to be indicated where (i) a provider can satisfactorily deal with the complaint without having to go to the Ombudsman Service and (ii) once the case is presented to the Ombudsman Service, the decision does not tend to go in the customer's favour.

These two aspects are summarised in Fig. 4.4, which combines the data for three six-month periods from the start of 2014 to mid-2015. Figure 4.4 shows the number of complaints in each six-month period along the horizontal axis, and the percentage of complaints resolved by the Ombudsman in the customer's favour, and against the firm, on the vertical axis.

Each point in Fig. 4.4 represents a single bank or building society group in one of the six-month periods. The number of complaints is unsurprisingly related to the size of the group, with big banks being the subject of most of the complaints the FOS received. On the other hand, building societies tend to be in the bottom-left corner of the chart, indicating that they have a relatively low share of complaints. Furthermore, this suggests that a low proportion of complaints are decided against the society by the

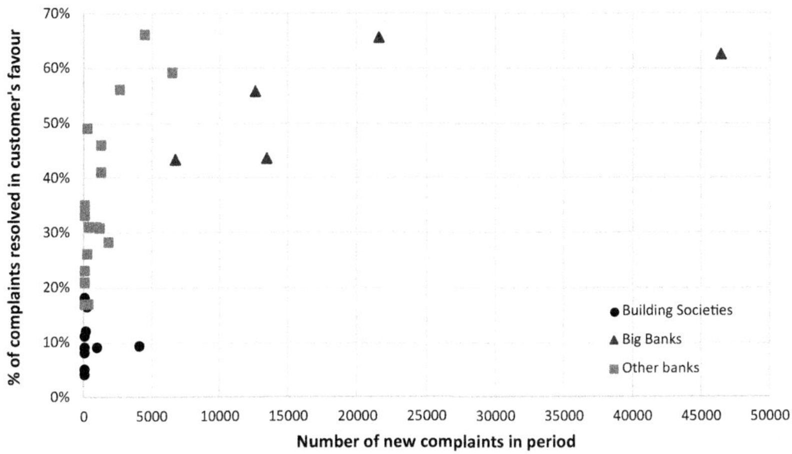

Fig. 4.4 Financial Ombudsman Complaint Statistics (*Source*: Data from FOS, authors' calculations). (Note: Average resolution rates at a group level are weighted by new complaints for each group company in the period)

Ombudsman. In contrast, many banks have a high proportion of cases that are decided against the bank.

The FCA and its predecessor, the Financial Services Authority (FSA), publish data on fines that they have levied on firms for misconduct. From 2010 to the end of 2015, there have been a total of 318 fines published to a value of £3.3 billion (see Table 4.2). These fines cover the range of regulated activities and therefore include fines on banking activities as well as fines levied on individuals and companies in fund management, financial advice, broking, and insurance. Totalling the figures, the fines levied on groups with retail banking operations come to £1.3 billion over the period, though over half of this amount relates to wholesale and investment banking activities (including the rigging of London interbank offered rate (LIBOR) and the foreign exchange market). Fines paid by banks in relation to retail banking activities only (including Payment Protection Insurance (PPI)) come to £0.6 billion.

In total, building societies received three fines totalling £0.007 billion (£7 million). Even drilling down into the figures to this level, it is clear that building societies have an extremely small share of the number of fines

Table 4.2 Conduct fines levied by UK conduct regulators (2010–2015)

	Number of fines	*% share*	*Value, £bn*	*% share*
Building societies	3	0.9	0.007	0.2
High street banking groups	30	9.4	1.4	42.5
of which relate to retail operations	20	6.3	0.3	9.0
Other firms and individuals	285	89.6	1.9	57.3
Totals	318		3.3	

Source: Data from the Financial Conduct Authority (FCA) and the Financial Services Authority (FSA)

and, in particular, the value of fines levied over the period by the conduct regulators. In addition, in the last two years, the Prudential Regulatory Authority (PRA) has also sanctioned three banks, fining two of them, but no building societies.

A major conduct failure that has become apparent in recent years is the mis-selling of PPI. This is insurance which covers a borrower's loan repayments under certain circumstances, if they are unable to make their repayments for a period (e.g. if they lose their job or fall ill). It can therefore be useful to give a borrower peace of mind, but it was found that for several years prior to the financial crisis, consumers were being mis-sold the insurance. The sale of PPI was not widespread at building societies.

According to the FCA, from January 2011 to October 2015, almost £22 billion was paid to consumers who had complained about the way that PPI had been sold to them. As well as payments for redress, a number of firms received fines relating to the original mis-selling of PPI.

Furthermore, to compound this mistreatment of customers, Lloyds and Clydesdale and Yorkshire banks received fines of £117 million and £21 million, respectively, for failing to treat customers fairly when dealing with their PPI complaints. The scale of these fines perhaps indicated that the FCA was keen to ensure that the redress and conduct fines did not become little more than a cost of doing business that needed to be minimised, rather than a risk that needed to be monitored and managed by boards of directors.

In late 2015, the FCA consulted on whether it should set a time limit on claims for PPI mis-selling, after which banks would not be liable for redress (the outcome of the consultation is pending at the time of writing).

The various statistics described above suggest that there is some systematic difference in the way that building societies treat their customers compared to other providers. It seems reasonable that this could be due to centrality of consumers as owners of the organisation. Policymakers should therefore give consideration to factors beyond price when assessing the effectiveness of competition in benefiting consumers.

4.6 Recent Political Support for Mutuality

Despite some troubles during the global financial crisis, the benefits of the mutual model relative to the more widespread mismanagement of banks, led to cross-party political support. The 2010 General Election manifestos of all three main political parties recognised the importance of mutuals. When the resulting Conservative–Liberal Democrat Coalition published its Coalition Agreement programme for government it pledged:

> We want the banking system to serve business, not the other way round. We will bring forward detailed proposals to foster diversity in financial services, promote mutuals and create a more competitive banking industry.
>
> (HM Government 2010)

During the subsequent Parliament, the Treasury published a discussion document titled *The future of building societies*, which put further amendments to building society legislation in train. This document had the aim of ensuring building societies "are given the conditions to allow them to thrive, while maintaining their unique identity and status" and set out the government's vision for the sector:

> The Government's vision for the building societies sector is of a thriving, independently minded and sustainable sector that is able to continue offering consumers a mutually-owned option for their deposits and mortgage lending. It is of a sector that stays true to the best principles of its history, delivering excellent customer service and avoiding unsustainable, risky business models. And it is of an innovative, developing sector, which is constantly seeking out new ways to serve its members and communities, while remaining true to its mutual values.
>
> (HM Treasury 2012)

4.7 Current Issues

Various regulatory reforms continue to be implemented: leverage ratios; firms' ability to absorb losses; risk-based deposit insurance funding; the European Mortgage Credit Directive; a market study of the Cash Savings Market; the Senior Management Regime and the Certification regime. The list goes on, and banks and building societies face a challenge staying on top of all the issues. It is particularly important that the reforms are implemented so that they are appropriate to mutual ownership and proportionate to the risk posed by individual firms, particularly smaller ones.

Many of the reforms introduced after the crisis have been aimed at reducing the Too-Big-To-Fail (TBTF) problem of banks, that is the assumption that the government could not credibly commit to letting a large institution fail because of its impact on the rest of the financial system. As a result of this implicit guarantee, large banks enjoyed lower funding costs. This gave them an unfair advantage and distorted the markets in which they operated. If the reforms are successful in reducing the TBTF problem, this should enable firms, including building societies, to compete on a more equal basis for custom. Increasing competition is also now a key objective of the prudential and conduct regulators.

At the time of writing (early 2016), only a small number of societies offer current accounts—Nationwide, Cumberland, and Norwich & Peterborough (a trading name of Yorkshire). Depending how regulation and new entrants affect the structure of the payments systems, this number may increase in the future.

The FLS has resulted in new lending and lower funding costs which have led to a recovery in building society profitability in recent years. However, intensifying competition in the mortgage market as the big banks return, and the eventual closure of the FLS, is likely to mean that the improvement in margins will not continue.

The BOE's MPC is generally expected to start to gradually raise interest rates possibly later in 2016. This is likely to have a positive impact on margins, as any outstanding tracker mortgages will follow the base rate increases and deposit margins are likely to improve. However, the increase in interest rates depends on the state of the UK economy and might be further delayed. In addition, the precise impact on banks' and building societies' profitability depends on how market interest rates will respond to interest rate increases. Furthermore, rising rates may cause some borrowers to struggle to meet their repayments and therefore result in a decrease in banks' and societies' profits due to an increase in non-performing loans.

It is expected that the Financial Policy Committee (FPC) will become a more significant regulatory body for building societies, as it applies housing market tools for which it was granted powers in 2015. From its instigation, the FPC has been clear that the growth of credit linked to the housing market is one of the most frequent causes of systemic instability. The FPC requested and was granted powers to set limits on new lending on mortgage Loan-to-Value (LTV) ratios, and borrower Debt-to-Income (DTI) ratios. The FPC had already recommended that a narrower Loan-to-Income (LTI) limit be applied in 2014: no firm should have more than 15% of lending in a quarter at Loan to income ratio (LTI) of 4.5 or more. The FPC is also paying close attention to Buy-to-Let lending, which has been a growth area for societies and banks in recent years.

Building societies have taken advantage of their recent strong performance to invest in new systems and technologies. Societies will have to continue to invest in and reform their businesses to incorporate developments in digital technologies and channels. Though in many ways we now live in a more individualistic society, with social media and mass communication representing fundamental changes in social interaction and collaboration, these trends could be aligned with the concept of mutuality if societies can harness the shared values of their member communities and integrate themselves in these networks.

Similarly, other approaches that are hailed as novel, such as peer-to-peer lending (also called loan-based crowd funding) where individual savers lend to borrowers without going through a traditional financial intermediary, have clear parallels with early building societies.

As such, the mutual ethos that is part of building societies heritage can be extremely relevant today. Building societies remain specialist retail financial institutions that are owned by their customers, as they have been since their origins almost 250 years ago. Their operations have evolved over time, and despite a shift in the structure of the sector with the demutualisations in the 1990s, the continuing societies have emerged from the recent recession in a relatively strong position.

However, for the sector to regain some of the critical mass that it lost in the period of demutualisations, new societies need to be formed. The Building Societies Act 1986 determines that a new building society can be established by ten or more people, and the capital which they have to put into the society is a minimum of £1 million in deferred shares. However, in practice, the investment required for the Information Technology (IT) infrastructure, branch network, branding, and so on will be far greater, before considering the need to obtain regulatory approval, making it difficult to see how it could occur in the near term. It may be that there is a need for public sector involvement or support for a new society to be established today.

4.8 Conclusion

The structure of the building society industry has changed substantially since the 1980s. Key changes were the demutualisation process, which saw the largest building societies transforming into banks, and the relaxation of restrictions on activities. The latter opened the way for banks to compete in the mortgage market. This resulted in a reduction of margins and encouraged building societies to expand their range of activities.

The sector was severely impacted by the global financial crisis, which forced further restructuring and consolidation. Although the number of building societies has reduced, the number of branches rose very slightly in 2014 as societies have looked to expand their operations, a very small reversal of a long-term trend. In addition, the number of people employed in the sector has increased.

In the post-crisis period, building societies have also increased their market share of new lending, partly as the big banks and other specialist lenders that had been active prior to the crash restructured their balance sheets. In addition, the number of borrowing members increased to the highest level since before the demutualisations. Some societies have increased their lending in limited ways into niche areas, such as self-build properties, shared ownership, mortgages for student housing, and parent-assisted mortgages (using a collateral charge over the parents' home to use equity built up in their property).

In recent years, building societies have also enjoyed political support as the importance of mutuals within a more diverse financial sector has been highlighted by policymakers and regulators. This support is also recognised by customers, as indicated by the high levels of satisfaction and trust.

Nonetheless, building societies face a number of challenges both due to regulatory changes and to technical and financial innovation, which are likely to have a considerable impact on the sector in the near future.

Notes

1. Note, however, that these ratios may be affected by the relatively high inflation rates in the early 1980s and 1990s.

References

Bank of England. (1990). Quarterly Bulletin Q4 1990 503.

Devlin, J. (2014). Trust and fairness in financial services: Summer 2014. Centre for Risk, Banking and Financial Services, Nottingham University Business School.

HM Government. (2010). The coalition: Our programme for government. Cabinet Office.

HM Treasury. (2012). The future of building societies. HM Treasury, July. Available at https://www.gov.uk/government/uploads/system/uploads/attachment_data/file/81426/condoc_future_building_societies.pdf

CHAPTER 5

The Performance of Building Societies: A Comparative Analysis

Abstract This chapter presents an empirical analysis of the performance of UK banks and building societies since the large-scale demutualisation process ended in the year 2000. Our results highlight the substantial impact of the financial crisis on the sector. Return on Equity (ROE) and Return on Assets (ROA) decreased for both groups in the wake of the financial turmoil, with 2008 and 2009 being particularly difficult years. However, as the UK economy recovers, the outlook is positive for both groups. Asset and loan growth are positive and the entry of new competitors seems to have had an encouraging effect on activity. Capitalisation ratios are above the regulatory guidelines and both groups are currently in a position to meet the regulatory minimum leverage ratio. Building societies in particular have recovered well from the financial turmoil, and they appear less risky than banks on a variety of measures, from lower volatility of earnings, lower volatility of net interest margins (NIMs), and higher z-scores.

5.1 Introduction

This chapter provides an analysis of the comparative performance of UK banks and building societies after the large-scale demutualisation of the late 1990s. In carrying out the analysis, we have focused on a number of metrics, which will hopefully allow us to provide an informative picture of the strengths and weaknesses of the different business models. In reading the results of the analysis, it is important to bear in mind that although

B. Casu, A. Gall, *Building Societies in the Financial Services Industry*,
DOI 10.1057/978-1-137-60208-4_5

they compete for customer deposits and in some of the same markets, such as the mortgage market, building societies have a very different purpose to that of shareholder-owned banks, as outlined in Chapter 3.

We are aware that assessing societies against standard bank performance metrics is unlikely to be appropriate and might yield a biased view of the sector's performance. However, we believe that this analysis will be informative for policymakers when weighing up what the future shape of the banking sector should be, if it can help to demonstrate the differences between types of organisations competing in the market.

5.2 Empirical Analysis

The analysis is based on a sample of UK commercial banks and building societies. The institutions comprising the sample are detailed in Appendix 5.1. For the purpose of the analysis, banks were further divided into Major British Banking Groups (MBBGs) and Other Banks. Building Societies were divided into three peer groups, according to asset size. The relevant ratios are presented both for the full sample and for the subsamples. Banking data are collected from annual balance sheet and income statements (unconsolidated financial statements) made available via the Bankscope database (Bureau van Dijk) and supplemented by information available from SNL Financial. Building societies data are made available by the Building Societies Association (BSA) for the purpose of this analysis.

Table 5.1 illustrates the descriptive statistics of our sample of banks and building societies. Banks are on average larger institutions, although differences in size among banks are bigger than among building societies. The sample is unbalanced to allow for entry, exit, and mergers and acquisitions during the sample period. We include all commercial banks and building societies active in at least one year over the period 2000–2014. To this end, each institution in the sample has been examined individually, for each year it was active over the sample period.

For the identification of the MBBGs, we follow the definition of the British Bankers' Association (BBA) and incorporate the changes in the definition over time. For example, MBBGs in 2000 included the following: Abbey National Group, Alliance & Leicester Group, Barclays Group, Bradford & Bingley, Halifax plc, Bank of Scotland, HSBC Bank Group, Lloyds TSB Group, Northern Rock Group, and the Royal Bank of Scotland (RBS) Group. The composition of these groups has changed during the sample period, following mergers and acquisitions (M&As)

Table 5.1 Descriptive statistics—banks and building societies (averages in £ million)

		2000	*2001*	*2002*	*2003*	*2004*	*2005*	*2006*	*2007*	*2008*	*2009*	*2010*	*2011*	*2012*	*2013*	*2014*
Banks																
	Number	**22**	**24**	**25**	**26**	**27**	**23**	**23**	**25**	**25**	**26**	**27**	**29**	**29**	**28**	**17**
	Total assets	**47,630**	**47,354**	**47,326**	**48,983**	**89,987**	**115,354**	**132,515**	**142,150**	**227,941**	**180,462**	**179,142**	**180,006**	**173,219**	**163,736**	**312,701**
	St .Dev.	*57,742*	*60,487*	*60,689*	*66,752*	*154,859*	*210,210*	*233,273*	*290,833*	*506,208*	*355,618*	*370,881*	*389,630*	*360,173*	*320,843*	*437,850*
	Deposits	**38,160**	**38,216**	**37,751**	**40,233**	**65,160**	**78,267**	**93,788**	**91,944**	**108,380**	**116,865**	**111,557**	**105,654**	**104,062**	**102,594**	**149,563**
	St. Dev.	*46,815*	*50,136*	*48,697*	*54,109*	*91,908*	*111,830*	*135,169*	*153,297*	*172,350*	*176,538*	*196,302*	*192,554*	*184,375*	*180,446*	*219,062*
	Total loans	**30,057**	**30,660**	**32,886**	**34,445**	**48,396**	**59,262**	**65,681**	**66,277**	**84,443**	**80,746**	**83,445**	**74,292**	**68,583**	**66,763**	**136,178**
	St. Dev.	*33,541*	*36,630*	*40,159*	*44,428*	*59,862*	*76,917*	*83,688*	*102,450*	*130,165*	*128,500*	*133,732*	*121,913*	*108,296*	*107,552*	*161,556*
	Fixed assets	**531**	**487**	**483**	**480**	**558**	**444**	**437**	**473**	**623**	**699**	**805**	**636**	**736**	**667**	**1,311**
	St. Dev.	*1007*	*984*	*1033*	*1066*	*1115*	*737*	*708*	*800*	*1153*	*1361*	*1498*	*1083*	*1394*	*1142*	*2160*
Building societies	**Number**	**64**	**64**	**64**	**64**	**63**	**63**	**60**	**59**	**53**	**52**	**48**	**47**	**46**	**45**	**44**
	Total assets	**2,369**	**2,652**	**2,855**	**3,246**	**3,749**	**4,261**	**4,907**	**5,262**	**6,555**	**6,371**	**6,447**	**6,556**	**6,953**	**7,052**	**7,398**
	St. Dev.	*8,278*	*9,224*	*9,694*	*11,122*	*13,205*	*14,728*	*16,338*	*18,534*	*25,083*	*28,147*	*27,860*	*27,878*	*29,260*	*28,834*	*29,168*
	Deposits	**544**	**599**	**594**	**781**	**1,029**	**1,207**	**1,368**	**1,578**	**1,985**	**1,634**	**1,564**	**1,498**	**1,619**	**1,578**	**1,502**
	St. Dev.	*2,153*	*2,105*	*1,867*	*2,475*	*3,626*	*4,072*	*4,313*	*5,466*	*7,711*	*8,168*	*7,958*	*7,686*	*8,197*	*7,476*	*6,695*
	Total loans	**1,808**	**2,008**	**2,178**	**2,480**	**2,905**	**3,338**	**3,872**	**4,158**	**5,087**	**4,798**	**5,057**	**5,158**	**5,480**	**5,867**	**6,356**
	St. Dev.	*6,187*	*6,889*	*7,360*	*8,522*	*10,436*	*12,034*	*13,498*	*15,449*	*19,985*	*21,592*	*22,174*	*22,077*	*23,043*	*24,154*	*25,559*
	Fixed assets	**24**	**26**	**27**	**29**	**31**	**31**	**30**	**32**	**36**	**36**	**41**	**47**	**51**	**57**	**57**
	St. Dev.	*91*	*93*	*98*	*104*	*112*	*115*	*98*	*108*	*136*	*155*	*186*	*218*	*242*	*270*	*273*

Note: For Building societies, Deposits include deposits and debt securities; Total Loans include loans and advances to customers; Fixed Assets include intangible + tangible fixed assets. Source: Data from Bankscope and BSA; authors' calculations and sector restructuring. In 2014, they comprised Santander UK Group, Barclays Group, HSBC Banking Group, the Lloyds Banking Group, The RBS Group, and Virgin Money.

For the allocation of building societies to Peer Groups, we follow the grouping of the KPMG's annual publication (KPMG Building Societies Database). The resulting groups (as of 2014) are as follows:

- **Peer Group 1 (PG1)**: Nationwide; Yorkshire; Coventry; Skipton; Leeds; Principality; West Bromwich; Newcastle; Nottingham; Progressive; Cumberland; National Counties; Saffron; Cambridge.
- **Peer Group 2 (PG2)**: Monmouthshire; Furness; Leek United; Manchester; Newbury; Hinckley & Rugby; Ipswich; Darlington; Market Harborough, Melton Mowbray; Scottish; Tipton and Coseley; Marsden; Hanley Economic; Dudley.
- **Peer Group 3 (PG3)**: Mansfield; Loughborough; Bath Investment; Vernon; Harpenden; Teachers; Stafford Railway; Buckinghamshire; Swansea; Chorely & District; Beverley; Holmesdale; Ecology; Earl Shilton; Shepshed; Penrith.

5.2.1 *Lending and Asset Growth*

Figure 5.1 illustrates the average asset growth of banks and building societies over the sample period. Although growth has been positive for both

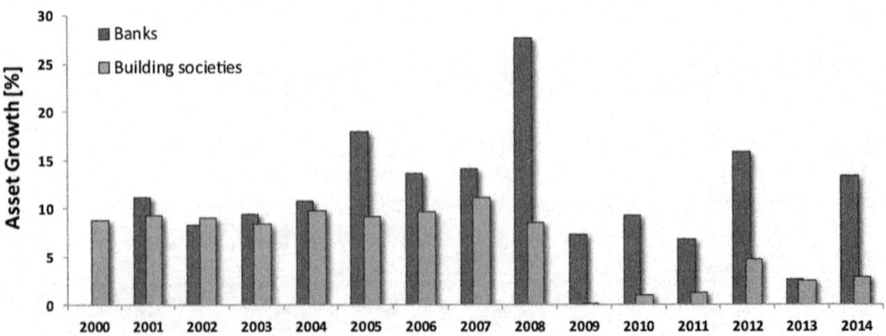

Fig. 5.1 Asset growth (%) (*Source*: Bankscope; Building Societies Association (BSA) and authors' calculations. The average asset growth for the two groups is calculated as Year on Year growth of individual institutions averaged across the group)

groups, banks have outperformed building societies in the run-up to the financial crisis.

The strong growth in the period 2004–2008 is driven mainly by the MBBGs, as detailed in Fig. 5.2. Note that the asset growth in 2008 is mainly driven by crisis-induced consolidation. Asset growth figures for Barclays include the acquisition of Lehman Brothers' investment banking and trading divisions, whereas the figures for RBS include the acquisition of ABN AMRO. Post-2008, the trend reverses for MBBGs, with the largest banks engaged in deleveraging and divesting non-core assets. The negative asset growth in the MBBGs group in 2013 relates to the divestment of TBS from Lloyds Banking Group and the continued restructuring at RBS. Indeed, the nationalised bank is currently half of the size it was in 2008, when it reached a £2.4 trillion balance sheet. RBS is winding down many of its operations in Asia, as part of a plan to retreat from many of its global operations and refocus on the UK retail and corporate clients. Although not with the same magnitude as RBS, other large UK banks such Barclays and HSBC have also been undergoing major reorganisation, with a view to cut costs and decrease assets. The positive trend among banks in 2013 and 2014 is mainly driven by new entrants in the market, including Metro Bank, OneSavings Bank, and Virgin Money.

Growth in the building society sector was also positive and sustained between 2000 and 2008. Although the general expectation is that asset growth for building societies is likely to be slower but more stable than for banks, there were nonetheless a few institutions whose fast growth outpaced the market. For example, between 2002 and 2008 Kent Reliance Building Society (KRBS) was the fastest growing in the sector. KRBS got

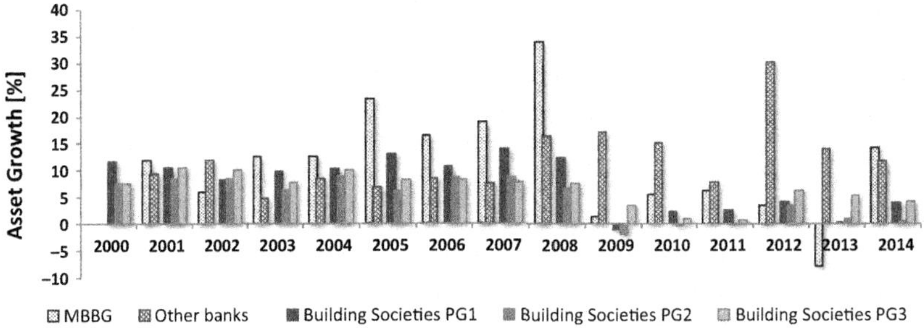

Fig. 5.2 Asset growth—MBBGs and Peer Groups (*Source*: Bankscope; Building Societies Association (BSA) and authors' calculations. The average asset growth for the five groups is calculated as Year on Year growth of individual institutions averaged across the group)

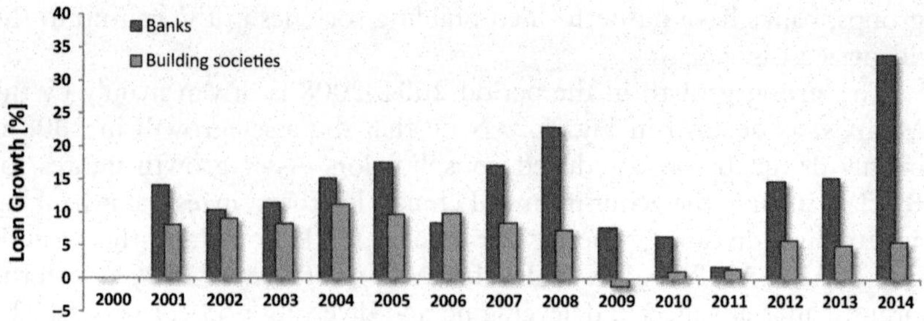

Fig. 5.3 Loan growth (%) (*Source*: Bankscope; Building Societies Association (BSA) and authors' calculations. The average loan growth for the two groups is calculated as Year on Year growth of individual institutions averaged across the group)

into trouble at the height of the financial crisis and in February 2011 it was transferred to a new financial entity, OneSavings Bank.

During the recession years, building societies' lending was limited. The sector, however, seems to have recovered from the financial turmoil faster than their banking counterparts, asset growth has been on average positive since 2010, although at lower rates than in the pre-crisis period.

Fast asset and lending growth are often considered as indicators of increased risk-taking in the financial sector. In particular, banks with high rates of loan growth in the pre-crisis period reported a more significant drop in their performance during the crisis (ECB 2010). Figures 5.3 and 5.4 illustrate the average rate of loan growth (year on year) for banks and building societies over the sample period.

Loan growth in both sectors has been positive and sustained over the period 2000–2008. Figure 5.4 illustrates the breakdown of new lending among the different groups. While average loan growth was mainly driven by the large banking groups in the pre-crisis period, a different picture emerges from 2009 onwards. "Other banks," in particular the new entrants in the market, record the highest increases in year-on-year lending, thus increasing their market share. The increase in new lending, illustrated in Fig. 5.4, has been mainly fuelled by these new institutions, as well as some strong performance by High Street Banks. On the other hand, lending growth, although positive in recent years, has slowed down for most building societies, particularly the larger ones.

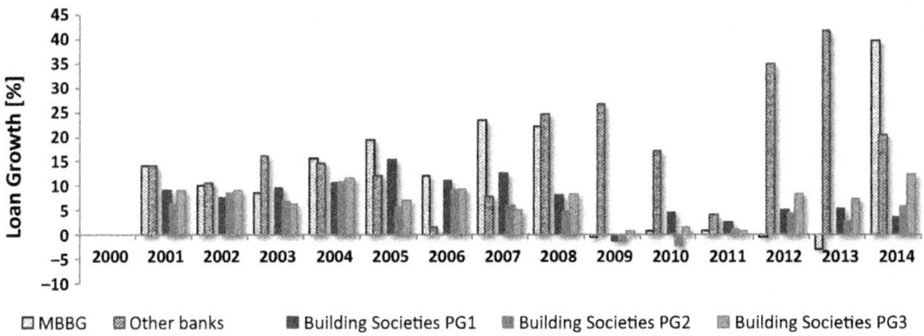

Fig. 5.4 Loan growth—MBBGs and Peer Groups (*Source*: Bankscope; Building Societies Association (BSA) and authors' calculations. The average loan growth for the two groups is calculated as Year on Year growth of individual institutions averaged across the group)

5.2.2 Performance Indicators

There are a variety of measures used to assess bank performance, with various stakeholders (e.g. depositors, debt or equity holders, managers as well as market participants, analysts, rating agencies, consultants, and regulators) emphasising different aspects of profitability. As we aim to analyse the comparative performance of banks and building societies, we need to take into account that each group of stakeholders and market participants has its own set of goals. To take these diverse views into account, we consider different indicators of bank performance: (i) traditional accounting measures of performance, ROE and ROA; (ii) a measure of the traditional intermediation function, the net interest margin (NIM); and (iii) an indicator of efficiency, the cost to income (C/I) ratio (Fig. 5.5).

ROE is an internal performance measure of the financial return of a shareholder's investment, and it is by far the most popular measure of bank performance as it relies on publicly available accounting information. It is estimated as net income/total equity and represents the rate of return to shareholders or the percentage return on each pound of equity invested. In order to carry out meaningful comparisons, it is necessary to note that most of building societies' capital is retained earnings, which do not need to be remunerated. Although building societies report the individual components of the ROE in their annual accounts, the resulting figure shows the rate of growth of capital, rather

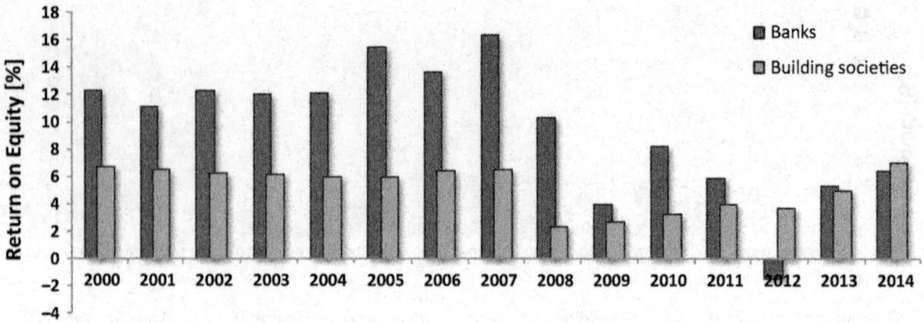

Fig. 5.5 Return on equity (*Source*: Bankscope; Building Societies Association (BSA) and authors' calculations)

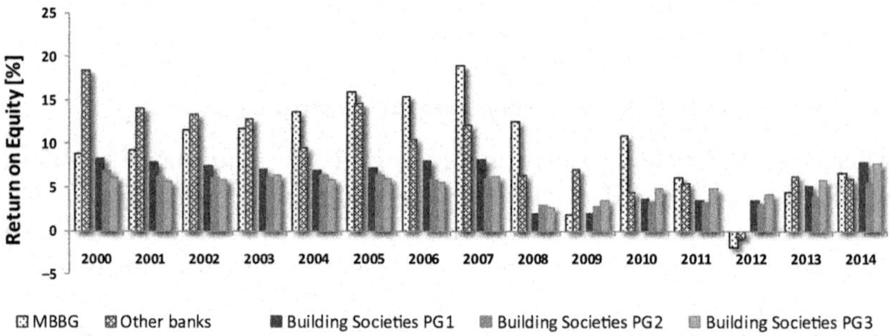

Fig. 5.6 Return on equity—MBBGs and Peer Groups (*Source*: Bankscope; Building Societies Association (BSA) and authors' calculations)

than demonstrating returns to investors. Though informative, building societies' ROE is typically expected to be lower than for banks. This expectation is confirmed by the figures displayed in Fig. 5.6, which indicate substantially higher ROE for banks. Large losses recorded by the largest banks, for example RBS, have impacted on the banking sector recent performance.

In recent years, the banking sector has not delivered the two-digit ROE that had become common in the pre-crisis period and have displayed returns not dissimilar to those of building societies.

A similar trend is found when considering the ROA. ROA is calculated as net income/total assets and indicates how much net income is generated per pound of assets. Again, building societies' ROA are generally

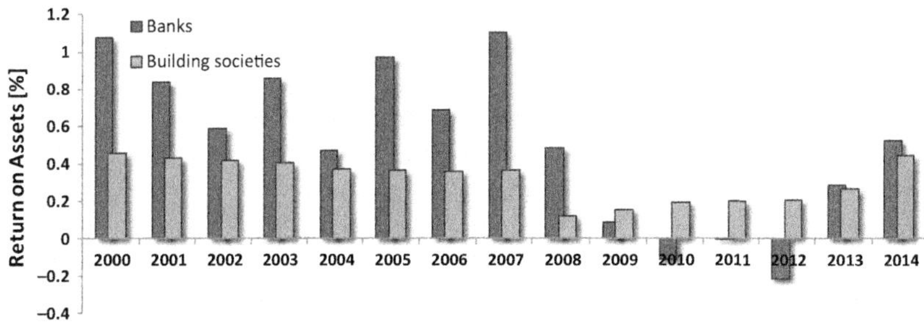

Fig. 5.7 Return on assets (*Source*: Bankscope; Building Societies Association (BSA) and authors' calculations)

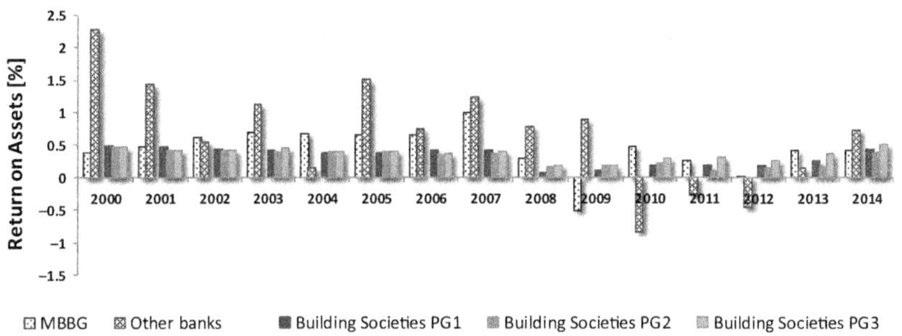

Fig. 5.8 Return on assets—MBBGs and Peer Groups (*Source*: Bankscope; Building Societies Association (BSA) and authors' calculations)

expected to be lower than those generated by banks, as they do not seek to maximise profits. This expectation is confirmed when looking at the pre-crisis period. However, unlike banks, building societies have been consistently generating positive returns on assets during the crisis and ensuing recession period, as illustrated in Fig. 5.7.

When considering the breakdown into peer groups (see Fig. 5.8), it is apparent that "Other Banks" have generated the highest and lowest ROA over the sample period. The literature indicates that while the ability to generate earnings is key to bank performance, it is also important to take account of the composition and volatility of those earnings to reflect the risk undertaken to generate them.

Measuring bank performance therefore requires analysts to take into account jointly bank performance and the volatility of performance. Figures 5.9 and 5.10 illustrate the volatility of ROE and ROA, respec-

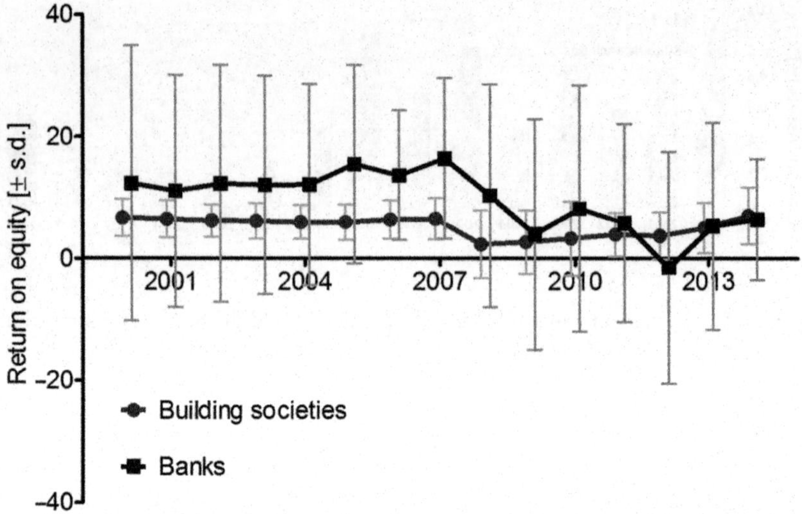

Fig. 5.9 Volatility of return on equity (*Source*: Bankscope; Building Societies Association (BSA) and authors' calculations)

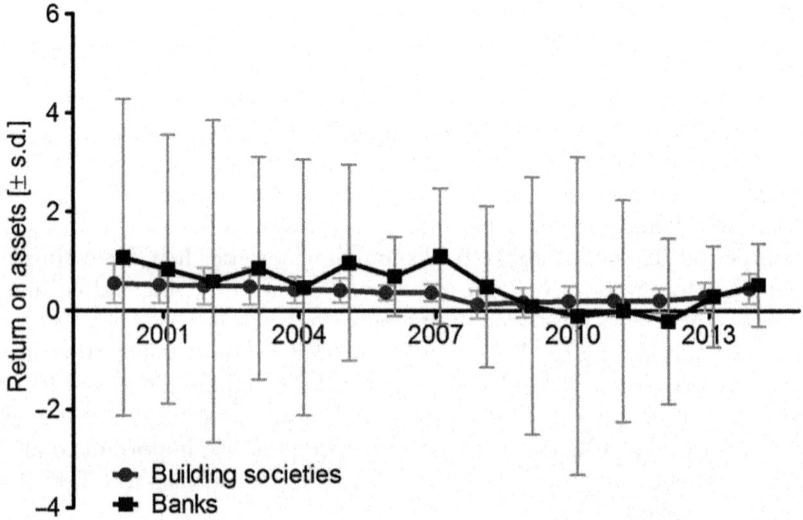

Fig. 5.10 Volatility of return on assets (*Source*: Bankscope; Building Societies Association (BSA) and authors' calculations)

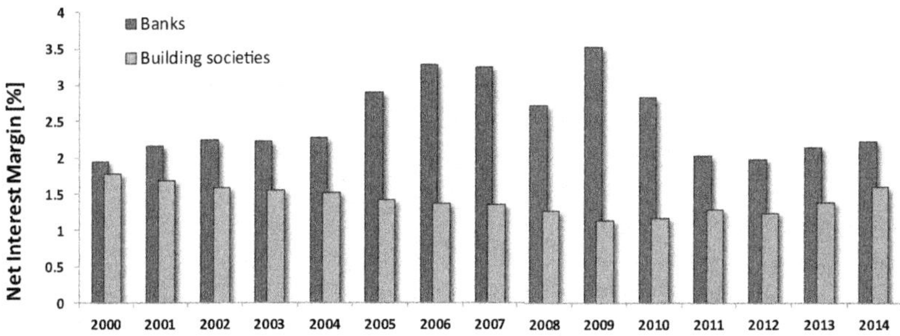

Fig. 5.11 Net interest margin (*Source*: Bankscope; Building Societies Association (BSA) and authors' calculations)

tively. While the average ROE is higher for banks than for building societies in boom periods (2000–2007), the volatility of returns (measured as the standard deviation of the sample ROE) is also higher (as indicated by the standard deviation of returns, captured by the vertical bars). Although lower on average, building societies' returns are more stable and, notwithstanding a dip in 2008, recover faster than those of banks.

The next indicator of performance we consider is the NIM, measured as the difference between interest income and interest expenses as a percentage of total assets. It measures the ability of managers to perform banks' primary intermediation function by managing assets and liabilities as to maximise the spread between the interest income earned on assets and the interest costs of liabilities.

Building societies will typically have a lower NIM than banks, as they tend to offer higher saving rates and/or lower mortgage rates to their customers, as a way to provide value rather than returns, and may have lower costs than banks as they typically offer a narrower range of services. This is confirmed by the trend illustrated in Fig. 5.11, as banks display consistently higher NIMs over the sample period. The difference increases over the crisis period and reduces from 2011 onwards.

It is important to note that NIM is also affected by bank risk-taking decisions, as riskier assets yield higher interest. A high NIM can be the result of a decrease in lending standards and derive from a risky loan portfolio. Or it can be the result of credit constraints and reduced availability

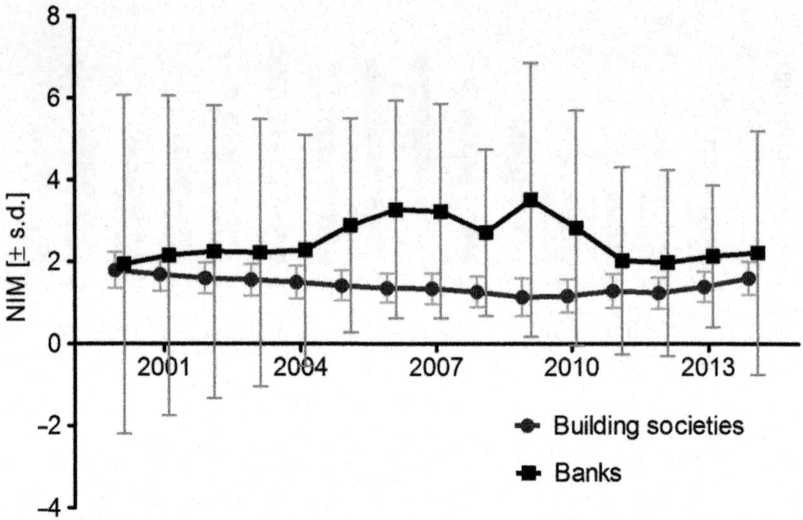

Fig. 5.12 Volatility of net interest margin (*Source*: Bankscope; Building Societies Association (BSA) and authors' calculations)

of credit. Therefore, the volatility of NIM is considered an indicator of bank risk.

As illustrated in Fig. 5.12, the volatility of NIM is also much higher for banks, driven particularly by "Other Banks." The MBBGs had relatively low NIMs up to 2004, although ratios increased between 2006 and 2009, at the height of the financial crisis. Conversely, building societies' NIMs have remained fairly stable during the sample period, with the largest changes experienced by the largest building societies (Fig. 5.13).

The C/I ratio is a quick test of efficiency that reflects non-interest costs as a proportion of income. Building societies might fare unfavourably on this ratio, for two reasons. On the cost side, most building societies are small and therefore might be unable to achieve cost saving deriving from economies of scale. On the profit side, as building societies are not profit maximisers, they might generate lower operating profits per pound of non-interest expenses. For an institution to be operating efficiently, the C/I ratio should be in the 50–70 % range, with higher ratios indicating lower efficiency.

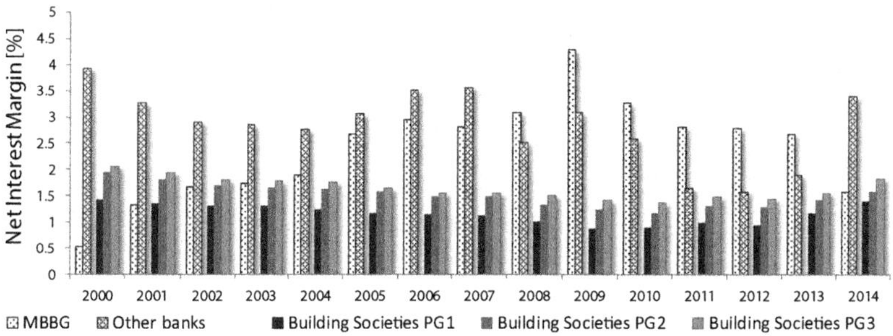

Fig. 5.13 Net interest margin—MBBGs and Peer Groups (*Source*: Bankscope; Building Societies Association (BSA) and authors' calculations)

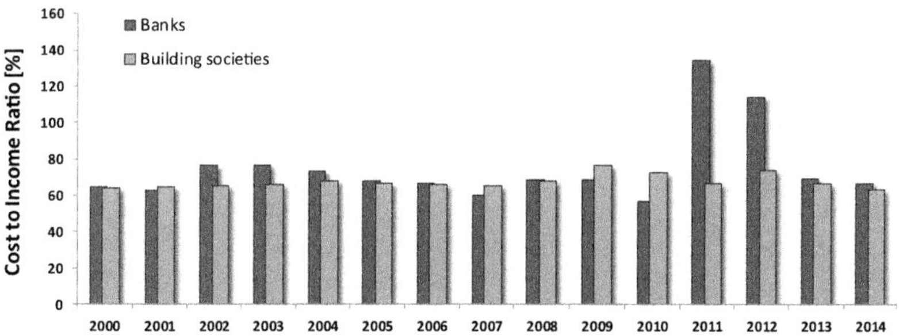

Fig. 5.14 Cost to income ratio (*Source*: Bankscope; Building Societies Association (BSA) and authors' calculations)

Contrary to predictions, building societies C/I ratios are not, on average, higher than those of banks, with the sector displaying good levels of efficiency and ratios around 60% on average during the sample period. Two new entrants in the market, Metro Bank and Virgin Money, who enter with initial very high costs, drive the increase in C/I ratios in 2011 and 2012 (Fig. 5.14).

The impact of the entry of new competitors is clearly illustrated in Fig. 5.15. MBBGs have on average lower C/I ratios compared to all other institutions in the market, as they steadily maintain ratios of around 60% on average. Other Banks have higher C/I ratio than building societies, on average.

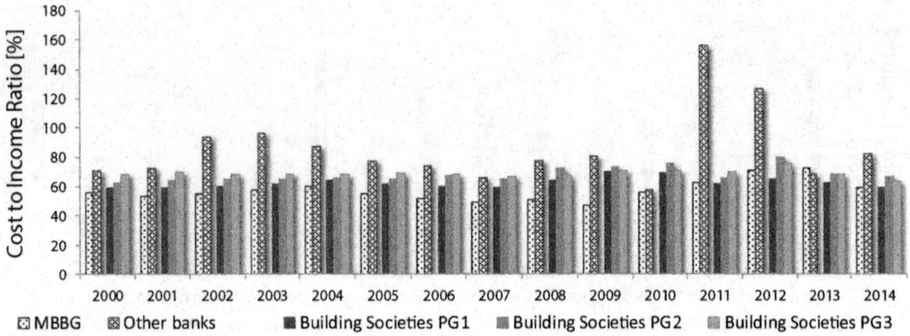

Fig. 5.15 Cost to income ratio—MBBGs and Peer Groups (*Source*: Bankscope; Building Societies Association (BSA) and authors' calculations)

5.2.3 *Solvency and Stability Indicators*

An evaluation of the performance of UK banks and building societies would not be complete without considerations about solvency and stability.

As building societies cannot readily raise external capital and rely on accumulated reserves they tend to have higher capital ratios compared to banks as they often accumulate voluntary buffers in excess of regulatory standards. In addition, most societies use the standardised approach to risk weightings in assessing capital adequacy (with the exception of Nationwide, Coventry, and Principality) (Fig. 5.16).

The new Basel III regulatory framework introduced a definition of leverage ratio as a capital measure over an exposure measure. The capital measure is the Tier 1 capital of the risk-based capital framework. The exposure measure relates to "total adjusted assets" that includes: on-balance sheet exposures, derivatives exposures, securities financing transactions (SFTs), and off-balance sheet (OBS) items. The minimum leverage ratio under Basel III is 3%, a figure that has been endorsed by the Bank of England (BOE) and is to become the basic minimum by 2019 for all PRA-regulated institutions.

MBBGs have, on average, lower leverage ratios compared to the rest of the sector. Large banking groups have been increasing leverage in the run-up to the crisis, while Other Banks are, on average, better capitalised. However, all groups meet the regulatory leverage minimum of 3%. The spike in the figure for 2010 for banks is driven by the entry of Metro bank, with a high initial leverage ratio, as also illustrated in Fig. 5.17.

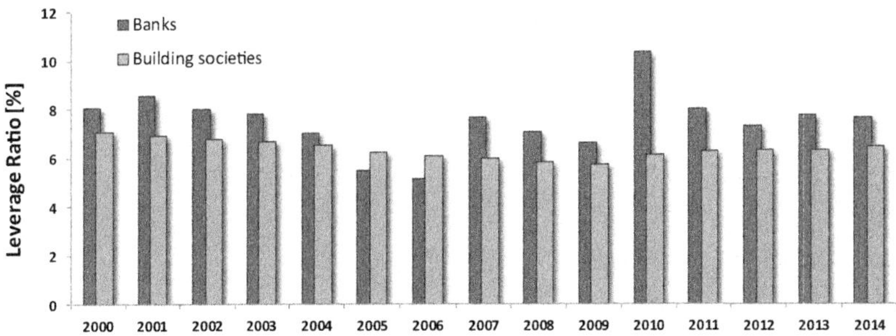

Fig. 5.16 Leverage Ratio (*Source*: Bankscope; Building Societies Association (BSA) and authors' calculations)

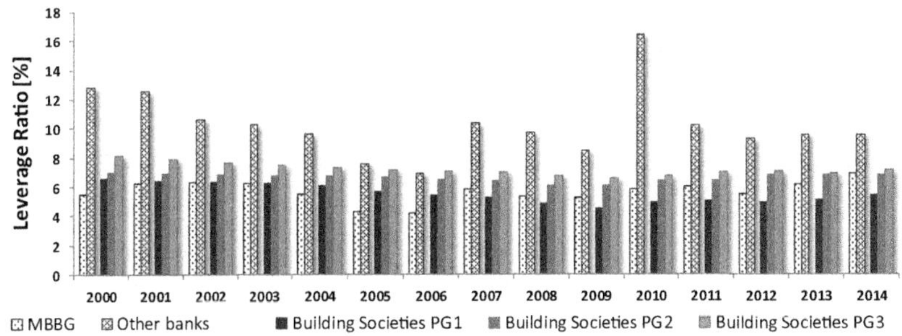

Fig. 5.17 Leverage ratio—MBBGs and Peer Groups (Source: Bankscope; Building Societies Association (BSA) and authors' calculations)

A snapshot of the regulatory capital position of banks and building societies, as per December 2014, is provided in Fig. 5.18. Building societies are, on average, better capitalised than banks, with Common Equity Tier 1 (CET1) ratios significantly above the regulatory minimum. The spread, however, is bigger than in the banking sector.

An increasingly popular measure of bank stability is the z-score, a measure of the distance from insolvency for a given institution which combines profitability, capitalisation, and volatility of returns. The z-score estimates the number of standard deviations that an institution's profits have to fall below its expected value before its equity becomes negative and is defined as:

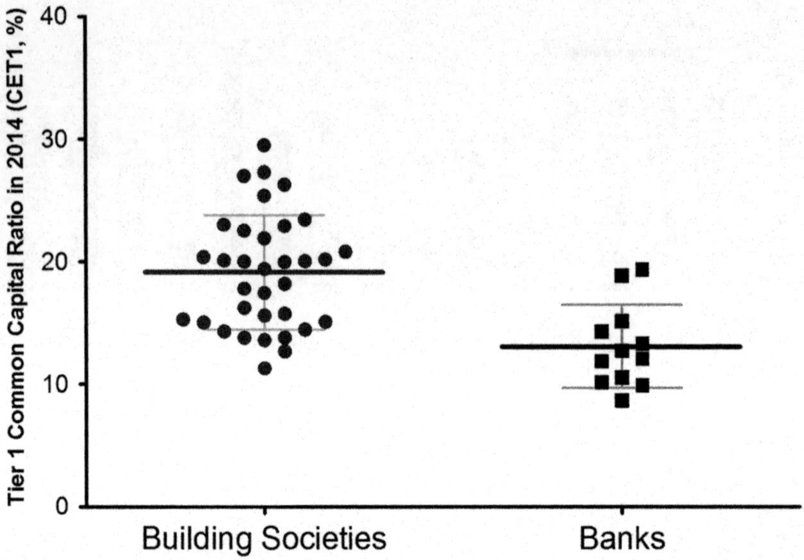

Fig. 5.18 Tier 1 common capital ratio (CET1) (*Source*: SNL Financial; Building Societies Association (BSA) and authors' calculations)

$$Z = \frac{\overline{ROA} + \overline{EA}}{\sigma_{ROA}} \tag{5.1}$$

where $\overline{ROA}$ is the average return on assets, $\overline{EA}$ is the average equity capital ratio, and σ_{ROA} is the standard deviation of return on assets.

A higher z-score indicates that a bank is more stable, or the less likely it is that the bank will become bankrupt. In other words, a higher z-score value indicates lower risk.[1]

Building societies are expected to have higher z-scores, as they are expected to have lower, but more stable earnings, and stronger capital positions than banks. These expectations are borne out by the results of the analysis. Figure 5.19 illustrates the z-scores of banks and building societies. The latter are significantly higher over the sample period although the gap reduces slightly during the 2007–2009 period.

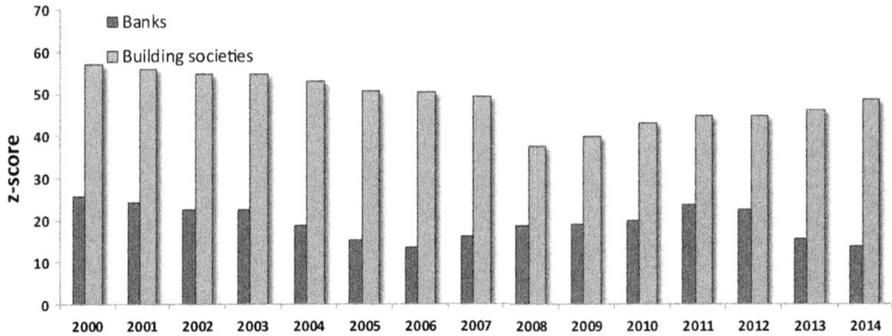

Fig. 5.19 z-score (*Source*: Bankscope; Building Societies Association (BSA) and authors' calculations)

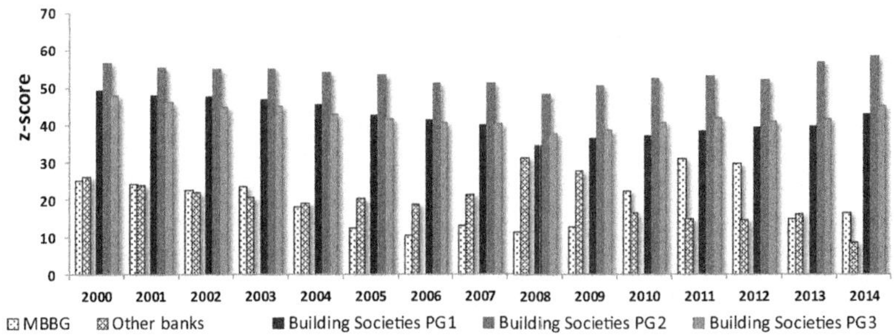

Fig. 5.20 z-score—MBBGs and Peer Groups (*Source*: Bankscope; Building Societies Association (BSA) and authors' calculations)

When analysing the different groups, MBBGs display the lowest z-scores (or the highest probability of default) during the crisis period, whereas "Other Banks" seem to have a highest probability of insolvency in the post-crisis period. These results are illustrated in Fig. 5.20. This is probably due to new entrants having a higher volatility of returns. Within the building society sector, the medium-size building societies (PG2) have the highest z-scores (or lowest probability of default).

In analysing z-scores, key information relates to the stability of the indicator with higher volatility indicating higher potential instability.

Although building societies have maintained, on average, higher z-scores compared to banks, the standard deviation of z-scores was much

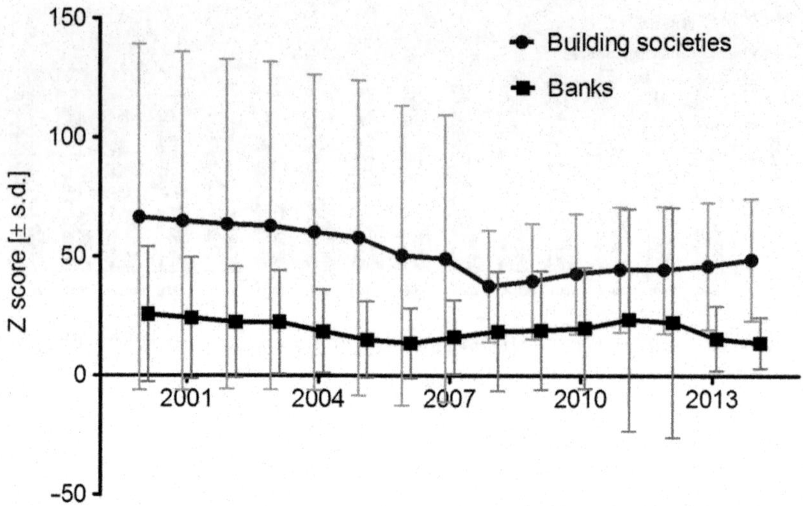

Fig. 5.21 Volatility of z-score (*Source*: Bankscope; Building Societies Association (BSA) and authors' calculations)

higher in the pre-2007 period (see Fig. 5.21). Remarkably, the building society sector has managed to reduce the volatility of z-scores during a period of increased market turbulence and have consistently outperformed the banking sector, in terms of financial stability, both with higher z-scores and lower volatility from 2009 onwards.[2] This indicates that the sector is in overall good health despite the challenging economic environment. With both the economy and the housing market showing sign of recovery, the outlook is very positive.

5.3 Conclusion

The chapter presents a comparative analysis of the performance of UK banks and building societies over the period 2000–2014. The results highlight the substantial impact of the financial crisis on the sector.

During the financial crisis, ROE and ROA decreased for both groups. Following the UK economic recovery, these ratios are positive for both groups. However, both banks' and building societies' profitability has not returned to pre-crisis levels. Positive indicators of the sector's overall financial condition are the positive asset and loan growth. In addition, increased competition and the entry of new competitors seem to have encouraged activity. Capitalisation and leverage ratios are above the regulatory guidelines for both groups.

Building societies in particular have recovered well from the financial turmoil and they appear less risky than banks on a variety of measures, from lower volatility of earnings, lower volatility of NIMs, and higher z-scores. Their recent performance should put them in good stead to face the challenges driven by regulatory pressure and reform.

5.4 Appendix 5.1 List of Banks and Building Societies Considered in this Report

Banks

Airdrie Savings Bank; Alliance & Leicester plc; Bank of Scotland plc; Barclays Bank plc; Bradford & Bingley plc; Bristol & West plc; Cheltenham & Gloucester plc; Clydesdale Bank plc; Co-operative Bank plc (The); Habibsons Bank Ltd; Halifax plc; HBOS plc; HSBC Bank plc; Julian Hodge Bank; Lloyds Bank plc; Marks & Spencer Financial Services plc; Metro Bank plc; National Westminster Bank plc – NatWest; Northern Rock; OneSavings Bank plc; Prudential Five Ltd; Royal Bank of Scotland Group plc (The); Sainsbury's Bank plc; Santander UK plc; Scottish Widows Bank plc; Secure Trust Bank plc; Standard Chartered Bank; Tesco Personal Finance plc; Unity Trust Bank plc; Virgin Money plc; Wesleyan Bank Ltd; Woolwich Ltd; Yorkshire Bank plc

Building Societies

Barnsley; Bath Investment; Beverley; Britannia; Buckinghamshire; Cambridge; Catholic; Century; Chelsea; Chesham; Cheshire; Chorley & District; City of Derry; Coventry; Cumberland; Darlington; Derbyshire; Dudley; Dunfermline; Earl Shilton; Ecology; Furness; Hanley Economic; Harpenden; Hinckley & Rugby; Holmesdale; Ipswich; Kent Reliance; Leeds; Leek United; Loughborough; Manchester; Mansfield; Market Harborough; Marsden; Melton Mowbray; Monmouthshire; National Counties; Nationwide; Newbury; Newcastle; Norwich & Peterborough; Nottingham; Penrith; Portman; Principality; Progressive; Saffron; Scarborough; Scottish; Shepshed; Skipton; Stafford Railway; Stroud & Swindon; Swansea; Teachers'; Tipton & Coseley; Vernon; West Bromwich; Yorkshire; Lambeth; Universal; Mercantile; Clay Cross

Notes

1. z-scores are based on accounting information and are therefore "backward looking." Chiaramonte *et al.* (2015) investigate whether z-scores are a good indicator of a bank's probability of failure and their results confirm that it is.

However, the indicator remains sensitive to the quality of the underlying accounting data and to the evaluation of the standard deviation of the return on assets.

2. The reduction in volatility is mainly driven by the fact that those building societies with very high or very low z-scores were also those that merged during the crisis period. For example, the Catholic Building Society was an outlier in the years prior to its merger with Chelsea Building Society in December 2008. Further consolidation ensued when the Chelsea merged with the Yorkshire Building Society in April 2010.

Reference

Chiaramonte, L., Poli, F., & Oriani, M. E. (2015). Are cooperative banks a lever for promoting bank stability? Evidence from the recent financial crisis in OECD countries. *European Financial Management, 21*(3), 491–523.

Index

B. Casu, A. Gall, *Building Societies in the Financial Services Industry*,
DOI 10.1057/978-1-137-60208-4

Printed by Printforce, the Netherlands